The Body

# The Body

Nick J. Fox

polity

First published in 2012 by Polity Press

Polity Press
65 Bridge Street
Cambridge CB2 1UR, UK

Polity Press
350 Main Street
Malden, MA 02148, USA

ISBN-13: 978–0–7456–5123–1 (hardback)
ISBN-13: 978–0–7456–5124–8 (paperback)


A catalogue record for this book is available from the British Library.

Typeset in 10.25 on 13 pt Scala
by Servis Filmsetting Ltd, Stockport, Cheshire
Printed and bound in Great Britain by the MPG Books Group

For further information on Polity, visit our website: www.politybooks.com

# Contents

# Introduction

One thing that I can guarantee about you, the reader of this book, is that you have a body! Not only that, but you are using its remarkable structures right now, to apprehend what I write. Our eyes, ears, fingertips and other sense organs constantly gather information about the world around us, and by nervous transmission (a process far more complex than electrical conduction), these sensations are sent to your brain, where processes as yet poorly understood enable the perception of what your body senses: the translation of the nervous impulses into an image, a noise or other representation of the objects that we are sensing. Other parts of our brain then interpret and evaluate these inputs, while others allow storage into memory or synthesis with other past perceptions to provide understanding. These processes may even lead to a motor response, a 'call to action' for our body (a smile, an utterance, going for a coffee). It is through our bodies (even if we interpose machines or other technology) that we interact with the environment around us.

The possession of a physical body, its mediation between the world around us on one hand and our internal world of thoughts, feelings and sensations on the other, is fundamental to the human experience. We experience everything as a consequence of being embodied, be it the sensation deriving from the sight of a sunset, the beauty of a musical composition, the touch of a lover, or the internalized cerebral processes that enable thought and the creation of a stable identity and personality. Our education, our emotional engagements, our experience of health, illness, care and pain, our physical interactions with objects, animals and other human bodies, our capacity to work: all are mediated by a physical body. Indeed, for many, it is the idea of being dispossessed of this essential resource that makes death so un-nerving a prospect: without a body, we seem to be nothing.

The physical body is a *necessary* precondition for embodiment (the fact and the experience of having a body). Everything you will read in this book is predicated on this assertion about the body. Critically, however, that is not the same as claiming that this biological basis is *sufficient* for our understanding. Or to put it otherwise, we cannot *reduce* embodiment to the physics of nerve conduction or the genetic codes in DNA that are needed to produce and reproduce an embodied human being.

Most of this book will be devoted to demonstrating that embodiment – having a body – is more than just anatomy, physiology, biochemistry and genetic make-up. We cannot discount these aspects of embodiment and I will begin my body odyssey by looking at the biology of the body. But I will also draw on those disciplines collectively known as social sciences: anthropology, psychology, sociology, economics, political science, plus some philosophy and other humanities. With the benefit of my undergraduate training in medical sciences and degrees in psychology and sociology, I will present to you the research that has been undertaken in these disparate areas to show the breadth of scholarship on the body and embodiment and confirm that, while biology is necessary for embodiment, it is not sufficient to explain the body's character. Other factors play a part in determining what bodies are, what it is to have a body, and what we mean by embodiment.

For thousands of years, humans have made assertions about the nature and character of the body and how to represent or 'tell the truth' about the body. These claims have sometimes not sat happily together, they have been rivals in cultural efforts to define and, indeed, control the body. At various points in history, one claim or representation may have been in the ascendant, at others, it has been subjugated by another in a struggle to claim the body for its particular perspective. Often these claims have been used to achieve control, not only of bodies, but of people's minds and allegiances, or to overcome or sideline resistance and dissent.

The earliest known example of a claim to represent the body happened when one of our prehistoric ancestors marked a cave wall with images of the human body. Some of these paintings survive to the present and may be seen in caverns around the world, from Creswell Crags in Nottinghamshire and Lascaux in France, to southern California, the Northern Territories of Australia and to many sites in Africa and Asia. When a cave-painter depicted the body of a hunter on the walls of her or his shelter, the body became not only a biological entity but also the subject of culture and a cultural object. Were these early artists using their paintings to record a success-ful hunt, to pass on techniques to their children, or to make a point about the conditions or the supernatural forces needed for a good hunt?

We can only wonder if these images played a part in helping our ancestors to think about their bodies in particular ways, to celebrate their physical forms or to mark their superiority over the animals they hunted. We may guess that the artist intended some meaning to be attached to her/his painting: for those who saw it to draw some conclusions about the activities of the human bodies depicted (perhaps it was simply a map to show a source of food, maybe something more). We still recog-nize these representations as telling a truth about the human body: about some salient features of its anatomical structure and capacities to interact with its environment.

Later artistic depictions of the human body offer messages that are clearer to us today, partly because they refer to sys-tems of thinking such as religion, philosophy, aesthetics and more recently science, that are still parts of our culture. Once humans became literate and used words to communicate, it allowed these systems of thought to remain accessible to us, even if the ideas are no longer accepted or credible. Early cultures set out rules for 'people with bodies' that circumscribed embodiment within ethical, religious or philosophical limits. Today's culture is no different, though the dominant ideas may have changed.

But consider for a moment a medieval depiction of the creation of Adam and Eve, the first humans according to Judaeo-Christian mythology. Artists may have shown God calling forth Adam from the dirt, or drawing Eve fully grown from Adam's chest. They may also have depicted the subsequent persuasion of Eve by a serpent to break God's laws and taste forbidden fruit, the couple's shame at their naked bodies and the expulsion of the transgressors from Eden: all bodily references. These depictions (and of course the stories set down in scriptures) set out an understanding of the human body for their viewers replete with religious and ethical messages: that the body was created by God from nothing; that female was secondary to male; that through temptation of the flesh, humanity had surrendered its rights to a life of leisure; and so forth.

The use of these images in places of worship reinforced religious claims about the nature of the body, perhaps to counter rival perspectives on embodiment from pagan cults that claimed the body as the source and site of pleasure and desire. When you see a painting of hell-fire and the tortures enacted on the wicked, it is easy to guess what messages the artist's sponsor (usually the Christian Church, but sometimes elements of a political state) intended to communicate, and also perhaps that such messages had to be hammered home so unsubtly because of unwillingness by many people to live a life of bodily abstinence and moral probity in the hope of deferred pleasure in the next life.

So, for the medieval European, there were some powerful religious assertions about the body, just as earlier cultures such as the pre-Christian Greeks and ancient Egyptians had their own cultural claims to the body and how it should be used aesthetically, ethically, sexually and so on. Historically, and in our own time, we can see the rival claims on the body played out between religion, science, art, social theory and popular culture, and the rise and fall of these claims. Most notably, modern, Westernized cultures have challenged religious precepts about sexuality, while science, psychoanalysis and social sciences have sought to re-define it in various ways (Foucault 1984).

The sexual body is hugely contested between these rival systems of thought and you and I – as individuals capable of reflection – have to choose from these rival claims as we decide how to live our lives and how to manage our bodies. Similarly, think about how we regulate our diets in response to rival claims about beauty, health and cultural stereotypes of body size communicated by popular media (Mennell 1991). While bodily illness is rarely associated now with immorality or malevolent supernatural forces but is broadly defined and explained by medical and biological science, lay perspectives remain influential and often contest medical understandings, with unpredictable consequences for disease management (Fox 2008a; Helman 1992).

Part of my task in this book is to describe the different ways in which bodies can be understood, and to summarize the disparate research that has been undertaken to describe the character of embodiment. With so many rival claims about the body, or representations of it, we need first to grasp what these rival perspectives are and their effects on our bodies. From this, we may recognize the differing biological and social forces at work, to understand why people regulate (or fail to regulate) their bodies, and how to resist or moderate these forces. This, you might conclude, is necessary reading for *anyone* with a body. But is it of particular importance for those working or studying in the area of health and social care?

The answer is yes, for the simple reason that health and social care professionals have bodies as the focus of their work. As a consequence of working with people who require health care or social care, they are involved in what we may call 'body work' (Twigg 2000). Whether their task is to diagnose disease; to provide physical or psychological therapy or social care interventions; to care for people while undergoing treatment in primary, secondary or tertiary care; or to help people to manage their lives and the consequences of illness, disability or ageing, in the community or in residential facilities, health and social care professionals work on, with or around bodies. While for many, their initial training may have majored in the biomedical disciplines, sooner or later they will recognize a need to understand the social, psychological, ethical, economic and political contexts of health and social care.

Imagine the following, if you will. We know that medical science has made remarkable advances in addressing fertility problems over the past forty years through a range of new reproductive technologies (NRTs) that help men and women who are struggling to become parents naturally. In vitro fertilization (IVF), gamete donation and implantation, as well as fertility diagnostic testing, all offer opportunities to enhance fertility, by addressing biological processes involved in reproduction.

These technologies have consequences beyond the matter of their practical application. For some people, it may not be morally or religiously acceptable to intervene in this way with a process that creates new human life. Ecologically, should we increase population fertility when the world is already overcrowded? Economically, should fertility treatments be funded by the state, if resources are needed to treat illness? If not, then is it acceptable that only wealthy Westerners should be able to afford to get reproductive assistance? And what of the psychological impact of fertility treatments: treatments such as IVF may raise hopes, only for them to be dashed if no pregnancy follows? 'Ovarian reserve testing' (which assesses how many eggs remain in the ovaries) may increase anxiety among young women that 'time is running out' for them to find a partner and start a family. What is the impact upon children who learn they are the products of reproductive technologies: how and when should they be told?

These are just some of the questions and issues that surround body technologies such as NRTs. They emerge because the body is not just biological; it also has cultural, psychological and symbolic significance, and is embedded within a social, economic and environmental context. While general readers may personally glean much of interest from recognizing the impact of these contexts on their bodies, for a health or social care professional the benefits will be in enhanced recognition of the character of their patients' or clients' embodied lives and the ways in which contexts affect health, illness and the life course, as well as improving or inhibiting the effectiveness of therapy and care.

The book is divided into two parts. In part I, I will present the range of perspectives on the body and embodiment that I have touched on in this introduction, starting with biological understandings and then moving to explore the main social science approaches. I will set out a way of thinking about the body that does not 'privilege' the former over the latter, or *vice versa*, but allows us to understand all forces on bodies in a similar way, by asking a simple question of great importance for delivering health and social care: 'what can a body do?' In the second part, I use this question to provide answers about the interactions between biological and social forces and their influence on our experience of embodiment, in terms of the life course and illness, desire and sexuality, discipline and body management, care and the effects of technology on our bodies' capacities.

So what is this body that we all possess and what can it do?

# CHAPTER ONE

# The Biological Body

A glance through the medical section of an academic book-
shop quickly reveals the vast amount of work that describes
the biological functioning of the human body. These textbooks
are the high-street tip of an iceberg of research in the biomedical sciences that fills the estimated 15,000 academic journals
(Manske 2007) in which scientists and health professionals present their findings and theories each year. This body
of research on the biological body is now so mighty that only
digital repositories can encompass it, as page by page, issue
by issue, these journals offer more detailed insight into the
biology of the body and its processes.

For more than two millennia, doctors, artists and philosophers have been documenting the structure and function of
the physical body. Since William Harvey's description in 1628
of the circulation of the blood, through Pasteur's discovery of
the link between micro-organisms and infection, to Crick and
Watson's modelling of the DNA double helix, modern scientists have set about developing theories to explain the workings
of the body as a biological entity and to apply these insights
to the treatment of disease and the enhancement of health
and life. Today, attention has shifted from gross structures to
the cellular and molecular levels, in the hunt for ever more
sophisticated perspectives on how the body functions, and vast
financial and human resources are devoted to this enterprise.

In this chapter I will set out the main ways in which biological scientists have appraised the body, and the issues that
arise from understanding the body as a biological organism.
I will look at some key ideas in the history of the biological

body, including evolutionary theory, and will also identify some shortcomings of a strictly biological view of the body. To illustrate the limits of the biological model, I will introduce the case study of Alice Martin, an older adult experiencing the effects of age and chronic illness. This case study will be used throughout this book, to bring to life the various themes you will encounter as we study the body.

## Science, biomedicine and the body

The history of the human race's fascination with the body and how it works pre-dates the modern scientific enterprise which informs the various disciplines of today's human biology. Most religions include an origin myth concerning the human body, while painters and sculptors have tirelessly represented the naked and the clothed body, in repose and at work. While science has brought a rigour to how the body and its structures and functions should be investigated, efforts to document, describe and explain the body go back to earlier eras. The fore-runners of what we now call the medical profession flourished in ancient civilizations, including pre-modern Greek, Chinese and Arabic cultures.

Modern doctors sometimes link their knowledge back to these ancients. For instance, the 'Hippocratic Oath', to which generations of doctors gave allegiance (although now usually replaced by concepts such as 'professionalism' and 'evidence-based practice'), recalls the Greek physician Hippocrates, who practised 2,500 years ago on the Mediterranean island of Kos, and is credited with theorizing a relationship between the body, health and the environment that influenced medicine until the nineteenth century (Fox 2011). Schools of anatomy and physiology grew up in ancient Greece; Chinese physicians developed theories of bodily function around the same period; while an earlier Egyptian civilization attempted to explain the functions of organs such as the kidneys and heart (Porter 1997: 50). The Greek physician Galen continued this tradition in the second century AD, while Arabic and Islamic scholarship from the ninth to the thirteenth centuries contributed to a corpus of work on human biology and medicine that informed a reinvigorated European interest in the body from the fifteenth century onwards.

To a modern eye informed by scientific medicine, many of the conclusions of these pre-moderns seem erroneous, far-fetched and sometimes bizarre. The purposes of the organs were often dramatically incorrect, compared with today's understandings. Galen believed that the heart was the source of vital power and body heat, while the liver created blood and warmed food in the stomach. Even the drawings made by the early anatomists seem fanciful to us, sometimes representing structures that owe more to mythology than accurate description. The artist and innovator Leonardo da Vinci's iconic portrayal of the human form known as 'The Vitruvian Man' subtly distorted the proportions of the body so it would fit his square and circle design. The sixteenth-century Flemish physician Andreas Vesalius produced detailed anatomical drawings that added enormously to understanding the body's physical structures and functions. Yet when it came to representing the female reproductive system, his depictions sought to demonstrate greater congruity with male organs than a modern observer would admit. His drawing of the dissected vagina resembles a clearly recognizable penis, reflecting a belief at the time that the female body was a divergence from a fundamental male form and, indeed, that the sexes were capable of morphing one into another (Herrlinger and Feiner 1964).

We can see features of today's scientific disciplines of human biology in these efforts to provide accurate and usable descriptions of the body's structures and processes. However, there is a discontinuity in this history, and we should not assume that the path to scientific biomedicine was simply a matter of progressively replacing error and superstition with rationality and truth, with today's knowledge of the biomedical body as the final, objective outcome. Science and the subject-areas that comprise biomedicine – anatomy and physiology, histology, biochemistry, genetics and the various branches of scientific medicine – are based on some fundamental perspectives about knowledge and how to acquire it that are quite different to the world-views that underpinned these earlier archivists of the body. To understand the biological (or biomedical) body, we need first to grasp how science works and how it differed from pre-scientific reasoning.

Around five hundred years ago, scholars in the West began to apply a new epistemology (a theory of how knowledge may be gained of the world and its contents). This epistemology, which formed the basis for science, was broadly speaking grounded in the notion that observational data (often obtained by experiment) was the key to gaining knowledge. By (and only by) reasoning from these observations, would it be possible to develop a theory about why something was the way it was and perhaps why it had come to be that way. This theory could then be used to predict events. Good theories would be useful and would come to be widely applied, while theories that did not predict successfully would be eventually abandoned in favour of more useful theories (though historians of science have shown that sometimes poor theories persist far longer than their sell-by date, for non-scientific reasons).

This scientific emphasis on observation and experiment replaced formal logic as the basis for theory. To give an example, Vesalius may have reasoned that if females were derived from a fundamental male form, then logically the female reproductive organs must resemble the male forms. Vesalius saw what logic told him he must see. The priority given to 'empirical facts' gathered by observation was intended to free scientific reasoning from the beliefs, customs and political affiliations that surrounded those individuals who were trying to make sense of the biological body. Scientists could describe what they saw down their microscopes or in a dissection, even when it contradicted the (often erroneous) authority of Aristotle or Galen.

No single date can be set for the emergence of scientific method. Some suggest a thirteenth-century philosopher and theologian Roger Bacon as the first experimental scientist (Clegg 2003); others nod to Isaac Newton as a champion of natural philosophy (as physics was then known). What is clearer is that the approach began to take hold significantly in Europe during the middle ages, possibly as a consequence of the emergence of humanism (the view that humanity is valid in its own right, rather than simply as the creation of a deity). This loosened the grip of a Catholic Church that had frowned on enquiry into the nature of a world and a body created by God and subject only to His laws. It also coincided with political changes that liberalized social structures and attitudes, improved access to knowledge, and opened the way to the idea that knowledge of physics, chemistry and other subjects could lead not only to understanding of the world (and the body), but also to improve the human condition.

The period known as the Enlightenment (around the end of the eighteenth century) was when science and its methods of enquiry based on observation and experiment really blossomed. Enlightenment philosophers, writers and artists set about a comprehensive re-construction of Western culture, with scientific rationality and methodology at its core, and earlier epistemologies including theology and mysticism sidelined. The industrial revolution provided a further incentive for applied science, in the pursuit of efficiency, productivity and consequent economic growth and profit. Political revolutions broadened access to power, and created an aspirational society that embraced knowledge as a source of wealth or control. During the nineteenth century, many of the disciplines (subject-areas) of modern science, including chemistry, ethnology and anthropology, geography and biology (plus the social sciences that we will look at in chapter 2), emerged as scientific enterprises as Western societies established empires and sought new ways to exploit natural and human resources. These disciplines together constituted an outlook that exists into the present, and is often summarized by the shorthand term 'modernity', in which rationality and science (particularly natural science) and its application are privileged over other 'ways of knowing', including literature and the arts, philosophy and theology. It has led inexorably to a secularized society, in which science and its applications dominate most aspects of daily life. Philosophers of science such as Karl Popper have described and refined an understanding of how science is conducted and set out principles aimed at maximizing its effectiveness as an epistemology and methodology, while excluding practices that might bias findings, or lead scientists into theoretical blind alleys (Popper 1959). Whereas once ethicists offered moral solutions to the problems of living, these philosophers set out rules for enquiry and the growth of knowledge.

The development of science is thus the backcloth for the biological body of today's health care professions. Despite the early example of Harvey's discovery of the circulation of the blood in the 1600s, it was only in the nineteenth century that medical professionals finally began to abandon their traditional homage to ancient physicians such as Hippocrates and Galen. Schwann's discovery of cells and the emergence of germ theories of infection in the nineteenth century began a move to embrace scientific theories and new technologies, based on careful observation of healthy and sick bodies, although Galen's humoral theory of physiology persisted as a basis for medical practice until the early twentieth century (Fox 2011).

In relation to the human body and physical pathology, the scientific approach has become known as 'biomedicine', linking the academic study of biology with the practice of medicine. The successes of biological science in accurately explaining the body's functions and enabling the development of effective therapies for diseases has underpinned medicine and other health care professions, and has formed the basis for technological advances in medical care (Clarke et al. 2003). As scientists replaced doctors as the source of wisdom about the biological body, pre-scientific medical theories gradually evaporated, and the medical profession belatedly adopted the scientific approach of observation and experiment. Health care is increasingly 'evidence-based', a phrase that summarizes the emphasis on observational data in science (Sackett et al. 1996). The success of biomedicine has also spilled over from scientific health care and health research into lay understandings of the biological body, as manifested in popular perceptions of health, body shape, development and ageing. The biological body has become the 'common-sense' body for most people.

This short chapter on the biology of the body cannot, of course, summarize the findings of a century of biomedical scholarship, or the content of those 15,000 biomedical journals. Over the past one hundred years, the biological body has been shown to be an immensely complex entity that must be understood at a number of levels, from the gross anatomical through to the molecular. Students of health sciences will be fully aware of the breadth of biomedicine from the reading they must undertake to gain knowledge of the subject-area! However, what is possible here is to focus on the 'top-level' theories that underpin a biomedical approach to the body. The first, which harks back to the Enlightenment origins of biology, connects bodily structure and function, while the second (concerning evolution) defines the way in which the body is understood in biological sciences and biomedicine.

## Structure and function

Scientific biology (or natural history, as it was called) emerged in the nineteenth century, with many of these early biologists or naturalists coming from the leisured or semi-leisured classes of Victorian society. With time on their hands, a gentleman or lady of this class might devote some effort to natural history, often resulting in vast collections of living or defunct specimens in their dusty studies, but also leading to thoughtful reflections on the features of these specimens and why they possessed these features. These amateur pioneers gathered insects, stuffed animals, or populated the private zoos of the wealthy and the new museums of natural history that sprang up in European cities. The more adventurous brought back exotic specimens from the corners of the empires that their military or commercial contemporaries were carving out from Africa, Asia, the Americas and Australasia. Fossil-hunters found evidence of animals and plants that no longer survived in living form.

Collecting and classifying these finds established the principles of taxonomy, including the 'binomial classification' of organisms into genus and species (for example, *Homo sapiens* or *Felis domestica*), usually based at that time on principles of structural similarity. Today, taxonomy relies more upon similarity at the level of genetic material, and species are periodically re-classified as their genetic differences from or similarity to other species are discovered.

But for the Victorian naturalist, a focus on structure also led to a fundamental principle of biology: that structure relates to function, that the way something looks is a consequence of what it does. Many of these early biologists were also church-goers, indeed natural history and a quiet country parish were mutually conducive pursuits for many a Church of England clergyman. So the elegant structure of a dragonfly's wing or the bright colours of a flower's petals illustrated the wisdom of a divine creator that made everything for a purpose. All things bright and beautiful: every structure needed to be explained. Imagine their questions. Why did a blackbird have eyes on the sides of its head, while an owl's eyes faced forward? Why did fireflies glow in the dark? Why was mammalian blood red?

To answer these questions required theories about the functions such structures might perform. Few amateur naturalists took the next step of devising experiments to test their theories and inevitably many theories were erroneous. A generation later, their successors in emerging university departments of zoology and botany had the resources to undertake the necessary tests to refine theory, and develop the methods of biological investigation that established academic disciplines in these areas, upon which today's biomedicine is broadly based. However, the principle that structure related to function first applied by those amateur collectors was what mattered and it is a principle that has weathered the emergence of a secular biology, in which God was no longer needed as the source of purpose, having been succeeded by a new deity, as we shall see in a moment.

The importance of functional explanations for a body's biological structures underpins modern biomedicine, whether those structures are skeletal, organic, cellular or even molecular. The heart has thick, muscular walls because its function is to pump blood and the walls of the left ventricle are the most muscular because this chamber has the task of forcing blood out through the aorta and to arteries throughout the body. The various internal structures of the membranes within mitochondria (sub-cellular organelles that perform key metabolic functions within an animal cell) and their precise chemical composition reflect the processes of oxidative phosphorylation, adenosine triphosphate (ATP) synthesis and the citric acid cycle that power cells.

Structures are explained by the functions that are progressively discovered by scientific enquiry, but at the same time, structures may give a clue to the functions of organs, cells or molecules within the biological body. Take, for example, the development of our understanding of DNA (the genetic material found in chromosomes) and its role in controlling a cell's biochemistry. In its crystalline form (as identified by X-ray crystallography), DNA adopts a double helical structure. The insights of Watson, Crick and Franklin linked this structure to regularities within the chemical composition of DNA and thus to theories about DNA's role in governing protein synthesis and also in transmitting genetic information during cell division (Watson and Crick 1953). Later work then confirmed these propositions and formed the basis for molecular genetics.

This two-way relationship between structure and function provides a basis for biomedical reasoning. A new theory of biological function may be justified by reference back to the structure of a body component such as an organ, a cell or even a molecule ('theory X offers a better explanation of the structural features than theory Y'), but also can offer clues which can generate hypotheses about a biological process ('the structure of this molecule suggests it has a role as a neurotransmitter'). This is true not only for 'normal' functions and structures, but also for deviations from normal functions or abnormal structural forms ('pathology'). Abnormal structures can be particularly suggestive of deviant biological function, while of course, the discovery of pathological processes can explain the structural forms (for instance a rash or a lesion) that appear as signs and symptoms in sick patients. I will look at the normal and the pathological biological body later in this chapter.

Over the past two hundred years, the level of analysis of the biological body has progressively moved from the gross anatomical structures of the body's organs, through the microscopic level at which cellular and sub-cellular structures and processes have been discerned, to the molecular levels that now inform biochemistry, genetics and therapeutics. As one level of structures and functions have been described and theories developed and tested to explain functions, the focus has moved to the next level of detail and complexity. However, the intimate relationship between structure and function remains as a characteristic of the process of enquiry, with molecular genetics, therapeutics and molecular pathogenicity (the molecular basis for toxicity and infection) all recognizing that even the structure of an individual molecule can affect its contribution to the normal or abnormal function of the body. The biological body has been rendered to its structural building blocks, but these are still related back to the body's functions in health and sickness.

## Evolution and the body

One nineteenth-century biologist who observed the structures of living creatures and speculated on the associated functions was Charles Darwin, a gentleman naturalist and geologist, whose travels in South America gained him invaluable data on fossils as well as a wide range of species of living animals and plants. However, Darwin took a different angle on the relationship between structure and function and drew very different conclusions from his findings. He focused on variations in form between species and speculated that the different structures they exhibited (one of his most famous studies looked at variations in beak-shape among species of finches in the South American Galapagos islands) could be explained by the different environmental circumstances of those species. Structure was related to function, but function was in turn related to the opportunities for a species to exploit a particular 'ecological niche': an environmental habitat that afforded better access to food, water, security, or some other attribute that could give it an advantage over other animals and thus aid survival of the species (Darwin 1859).

Thus the long neck of the giraffe might be explained by the potential to harvest nutritious shoots high on savannah trees, beyond the reach of other grazing animals. The camel's hump allows it to store fat, enabling it to colonize deserts where other mammals cannot survive. Both the opposable thumbs and large cranial capacity of *Homo sapiens* reflect the advantages humans gained over other primates from using tools to manipulate the environment.

Darwin was not the first naturalist to have evaluated structures in terms of environmental advantage, or to see this as the way that species adapted over generations, some species dying out as environmental conditions changed, while others flourished as they adapted successfully to their ecological niche. However, his insight was to propose a process of *natural selection*, whereby those individuals who were best suited to the environment survived to pass on their advantage to their offspring, while those less well adapted to it did not. Unlike some of his contemporaries, Darwin did not believe adaptation (the process by which the body's form changes over time) was a consequence of characteristics acquired during an individual's lifetime and passed on to future generations, but rather of random mutations acquired during reproduction. If a mutation made an individual more suited to the environment, that individual would flourish and reproduce. If another mutation created an individual less well-fitted to the environment, it would perish and not pass on that mutation to a future generation.

Evidence for evolution has grown since Darwin's insight, although it is only with the discovery of how genes code for a species' biological characteristics that the mechanism for random mutations to be passed on from generation to generation has finally been understood. Modern genomics has found a change to one single 'letter' in the DNA code can alter an individual's appearance or metabolism by switching on a gene, making biology far more mutable than anyone could have imagined. Evolution, once thought to take millions of years, has been found to sometimes occur in just a few years, when dramatic environmental changes (for example, a drought or a new predator) threaten a population.

The implications of this theory of natural selection are immense and are implicit in the modern biological model of the body. The evolutionary perspective enhances the structure/function relationship, offering explanations of *why* bodies have the biology they do: humans (and other animals) have a certain body shape, skin colour, erect gait, large brain and so forth for a reason. These features, according to evolutionary theory, are not a chance event, nor because we were made in God's image, but because we have successfully adapted to our environment. Our bodies provide us with the means to successfully occupy and exploit a specific ecological niche (albeit, in the case of humanity, one that covers most of the planet). The overwhelming success of humans in colonizing the Earth (through our ability to develop and exploit technologies) is testament within evolutionary theory to how well-suited our bodily structures are to the environment.

Coupled with molecular genetics (the study of DNA and how it codes a species' features), evolutionary theory establishes biomedicine with a strong narrative claim to explain the body and how it works. From this perspective, a species can be summarized by the sequence of 'letters' (representing the molecular 'base-pairs' within the gene) carried by its DNA. This sequence has been decoded for many animal, plant and bacterial species, including humans, and the human genome provides all the information needed to produce a human being. A human, a cat, a giraffe, a banana, or a flu virus have the characteristics they do because they have evolved to exploit their environmental niches, yet the process of evolution is entirely impersonal: the result of random (but beneficial) mutations over many generations that have led to the forms we see in the creatures living today.

This kind of 'biological determinism' claims that the body can be fully explained (determined) by its DNA sequence. Every physical characteristic down to a skin blemish, every variation in metabolism that may determine enzyme levels or hormone deficiencies, every susceptibility to or immunity from a disease or an infective agency, might be explained by the genetic sequence. The next step, of course, is to alter that sequence, to improve immunity to a virus or a cancer, to lower blood pressure, to protect against onset of degenerative diseases. What has already been achieved for genetically modified (GM) plants and cloned animals such as mice and sheep might also be done to human bodies, to protect and 'improve' the species. Gene therapy is a growth area for modern biomedicine, exploiting technologies such as stem cells that can be used to replace cells carrying 'faulty' DNA, while it is only a matter of time before a human body is cloned to produce its identical copy.

Evolutionary theory has also been applied in another way. If a body's structures and processes are a consequence of evolution of a species to best fit it to the environment, might not evolution have also been at work in determining human behaviour and psychological processes? Evolutionary psychology (and its earlier manifestation, sociobiology) is a field of study that argues that many aspects of personality and human behaviour (and consequently human culture and social organization) are 'hard-wired' into our DNA as a result of many generations of evolution. For example, empathy (the capacity to put yourself in another person's shoes), co-operative behaviour and creativity (the ability to use imagination to produce art, ideas, or tools) are all – according to this theory – beneficial behaviours or personality traits that have evolved to enhance the success of the human species, as may be our emotions: falling in love, jealousy, anger and so forth (Tooby and Cosmides 2005). The theory further suggests that those individuals who (due to genetic mutations) do not possess these characteristics will tend to die out, as they will be less successful and may not mate and pass on their genes to their offspring. Human behaviour and personality is thus the outcome of many generations of natural selection. Think about aspects of your own behaviour: might these have been influenced by your genes and even inherited from past generations?

Evolutionary psychology remains controversial, especially when it has been used to justify differences in sexual behaviour between men and women, or differences in personality or intelligence between ethnic groups. The possibility that these differences are genetic rather than a consequence of either an individual's upbringing or education can seem disempowering or unjust. I will consider some of the criticisms of an evolutionary approach to human behaviour later in this chapter.

## The normal and the pathological: the biomedical model

Over the past 150 years, medicine has fully adopted the principles of the biological sciences, so that we can now speak of 'biomedicine' and a 'biomedical model' of health and illness.

The biomedical model locates physical diseases within the body and assumes that they can be reduced to disordered bio-chemical or physiological processes (Freund, McGuire and Podhurst 2003: 6). The body, according to this model, is like a machine and disease represents a malfunction in its workings (ibid.: 7). This medical model has informed many of the health sciences, although some have been more critical, and sought a more holistic approach to understanding health and illness.

Biomedicine is an applied science, linked implicitly to the practical actions of health professionals as they seek to diagnose and overcome the effects of disease in their patients. Perhaps because of the authority of the medical professional, this scientific, biomedical approach has become the dominant perspective on the human body in modern Western cultures, and has made extensive inroads into lay perceptions, to the extent that the 'common-sense' body of the lay public is also the body of biomedicine (Clarke et al. 2003). Indeed, Deleuze and Guattari (1984) have called the biological body 'the body-*with*-organs': a body fully described and explained by biomedical concepts such as organs and cells.

I will have much more to say about the body-*with*-organs and alternative bodies later in this book. But for now I want to focus on one aspect of the biomedical body. Biomedicine and the biomedical model are founded on an opposition between the 'normal' and 'pathology' (literally: an abnormality causing suffering). However, whereas the 'pure' biological sciences recognize diversity of structures and functions as a feature of the natural world, biomedicine, because of its applied emphasis upon disease, actually privileges the pathological or aberrant case over the typical or 'normal'. What this means is that, whereas the early naturalists collected and classified typical or 'normal' specimens and noted diversity within and among species, health professionals collect and classify diseases and pathologies. In the biomedical model, where disease is the focus, then 'normality' (which equates to 'health') is defined only as the *absence of disease*.

This inversion of pathology and normality makes biomedicine and the biomedical body unique. Normal/abnormal
typologies of physical bodies are widespread, both across cultures and throughout history. In the next chapter, I will look
at the meanings of the body, but it is worth noting here that in
many cultures and even to this day, a physical divergence from
a cultural norm of body shape, size or form may have significance beyond itself. Bodily deformity and disability have been
associated with inherent wickedness or immorality, or seen as
a punishment for sins (Brammall 1996). For the unfortunate
individual, it could mean life as an outcast, or survival only as
an object of fear, distaste or laughter. In these typologies, 'normality' is privileged and any divergence is also *deviance* (a term
that implies a breach of acceptable behaviour). Deviance may
be severely punished in many societies, both in terms of legal
retribution for breach of laws and sanctions by social groups
against those breaking with convention or norms of behaviour. The sociologist Goffman (1970) described the 'stigma'
that affects those with a visible deviance such as a disability
(for instance, use of a wheelchair or a hearing aid), or deformity such as a birthmark or missing limb. At various points in
history, diseases such as cancer, epilepsy and AIDS have been
stigmatizing, creating a 'double handicap' for those suffering
from such conditions.

Since the era of Hippocrates, medicine had an aspiration
not to pre-judge the sick, disabled or deformed in this way,
but to devote itself to treating disease. Pre-scientific medicine
was not immune from its cultural contexts, and the concepts
used by the early medical professions were based more upon
general beliefs about the world and its nature than upon
sound knowledge, limiting the effectiveness of medical care.
The emergence of a scientific or biomedical model of disease
finally provided health care professions with an opportunity to
analyse the body entirely in terms of biological science, without recourse to external evaluations or judgements. Health
care based on observation and experiment to test hypotheses

(theories) enhanced its efficacy as a therapeutic enterprise and contributed to the authority of health professionals to be able to 'speak the truth' about the body.

While use of biological science freed health care from cultural judgements and beliefs about the body, it also limits its capacity to recognize contexts of disease (the subject of the next chapter). Biomedicine's privileging of pathology, to the extent that the normal can be defined only as the absence of pathology, and health as the absence of illness, inverts the relationship between health and disease seen in virtually every other cultural setting. This approach offers some advantages over non-scientific approaches to health and illness, but also has consequences that I will now consider.

## Criticisms of the biological approach to the body

The features of the biological model of the body that I have highlighted in this chapter provide some key criticisms of the biological model of the body.

The first limitation relates to the structure/function relationship that underpins biological science. We have seen that this relationship is used in two ways. First, a body structure may be used as justification for a proposed theory of body process or function. For example, the microscopic structures of sub-cellular organelles (for example, mitochondria and ribosomes) may be used to support theories of their functions within cells (energy conversion and protein synthesis, respectively). Second, a structure may give clues to function. For instance, mitochondria contain DNA and resemble bacterial cells, so some theorists believe they were originally bacteria that were swallowed up by larger cells. In both cases, the structure/function relationship is seductive: we want to believe that these two aspects are related, because it appeals to a desire for rationalism in nature. Once people argued that the elegance of creation was evidence for a rational God, now a nature in which body structures are entirely suited to the functions of those structures offers the assurance that nature is logical or coherent. Watson, the co-discoverer of the function of DNA, said that the structure of DNA's double helix was 'so pretty it had to be true'! (Watson 1968: 134).

Structures no doubt are often, perhaps usually, reflections of a body's function. However, the risk is that if this relationship is assumed, it may bias biology and biomedicine towards particular theories. It may be that the clues we get from structures are erroneous, and will lead to inaccurate or even dangerous theories, or that the evidence of structure is over-estimated and precludes other rival theories. This leads to a tendency to *biological determinism*, in which biology is privileged over other factors that may affect bodies. Physical structures come to hold too much significance in understanding what bodies are and what they do. For example, a mechanical model of the body may over-emphasize the similarity with a machine, ignoring the capacity of organisms to grow, learn and adapt to circumstances. Nineteenth-century doctors believed the shape of the skull affected personality: which of today's theories of structure and function may turn out to be similarly erroneous?

Evolutionary theory and molecular genetics, perhaps ironically, undermine a belief in the internal consistency of nature. Tiny mutations in a person's DNA can alter their eye colour from brown to blue, determine the extent to which a gene governing facial anatomy is expressed, or affect susceptibility to a disease. This mutability is random, down to accidental changes in DNA that may or may not benefit an individual. There is no logic to evolution: it occurs randomly, and species and individuals survive or die out as a consequence of how chance events at a molecular level fit them to the environment at that point in time. Molecular biology has refined the structure/function relationship to the extent that a few atoms in a gene can determine part of a body's structure. This may be seen as *biological reductionism*, in which body function is reduced to the level of the molecule and random mutation. This reductionism is most evident in the case of evolutionary psychology discussed earlier, where even personality traits and human behaviour are reduced to genetics, ignoring the potential effects of environment and upbringing.

Evolutionary theory is also prone to the criticism that it cannot easily be disproved. While there is growing evidence that adaptation to the environment occurs, and can occur very rapidly, we cannot go back in time and confirm how well a fossil animal or plant fitted its environment. It is inevitably speculation that changes in the environment led to one species dying out and new species evolving. This criticism is most potent in relation to claims that human behaviour, personality characteristics and even sexual attraction have evolved to enable humans to exploit their environment. Such arguments can be developed to substantiate any aspect of behaviour. For instance, honesty could be evolutionarily important for a collaborative and social species such as our own. Yet contrary behaviours can also be justified. Thus, lying could be a useful attribute, giving the untruthful an advantage (for example, in gaining a mate) in a generally honest society. This kind of spurious reasoning also leads to biological reductionism, as it enables more and more of embodied life to be explained by evolution and the genetic code. Try to come up with your own theories of how behaviour (for instance, 'falling in love' or following the latest fashion) might have evolutionary advantage. Then see if you can also argue the opposite!

The third shortcoming of the biological approach concerns its application in medicine. As was noted, biomedicine has taken the biological body and imposed its own inversion on it, so that disease and pathology become the prime focus, and 'health' comes to be simply the absence of disease. For health care, this has the consequence of focusing attention upon biological processes, and away from the more experiential aspects of well-being. The medical model struggles to incorporate non-biological elements (for example, how social contexts may affect how health and health care are experienced) and tends toward biological determinism, reductionism or both.

Given the importance accorded to biomedical models in popular understanding of the body, the medical model 'seeps' into non-health related aspects of embodiment (for example, sexuality, education and even criminology). There is often recourse in popular discussions of these areas to apply biologically deterministic or reductionist arguments, so that – for example, poor educational progress is put down to attention deficit disorder, or a gene to explain the amoral behaviour of criminals is proposed. See if you can find other examples in the popular media of this kind of biomedical determinism. The attractive ideas of the structure/function relationship and evolution may offer temptingly simple explanations of behaviour and personality that actually require more subtle answers than biomedicine has on offer.

## A case study: chronic illness and the biological body

To conclude this chapter, I will now introduce the case study that will be used throughout this book. I will show here how the biological body offers some explanations of chronic illness, but is limited and needs augmenting with other perspectives.

Chronic illness has overtaken acute diseases (such as infections and work-related diseases) in the developed world. As people live longer, living conditions have improved, and more therapies to treat common infectious diseases have led to immunization and other preventive measures, the diseases afflicting populations have shifted to those with onset in middle-life, such as heart disease, diabetes and degenerative diseases such as dementias and bone and joint conditions. People with these diseases will live with them for twenty, thirty or more years, and many are not fatal, though they may have major impacts on function and quality of life.

Take Alice Martin (an entirely invented person), for example. Alice is 75 and suffers from osteoarthritis, a joint disease associated with ageing. She first experienced symptoms in her early sixties, and the disease has progressively affected more and more of her joints, including knees, hips and spinal column. Her therapy comprises medicines to reduce the pain of the disease and she had a knee replacement operation five years ago. She is now under consideration for one or both hip replacements. She attends a bone and joint clinic once every six months, to 'tweak' her medication and ensure she is gaining the benefit of advances in chemotherapy. For Alice, arthritis is part of her daily life. She has accommodated to it, but it does significantly affect her capacity to perform many normal daily functions including walking, cooking and driving. The pain of the disease sometimes gets her down and she fears she will eventually be house-bound, or have to move into a ground-floor apartment. Alice is keen to be involved in her treatment and actively seeks out information. She is a member of the local arthritis support group and also collects money for an arthritis charity. She was widowed three years ago and has two children who live at a distance.

What can we learn about Alice and her condition from the biological approach to the body? The biology of arthritis is relatively well understood and, in the case of osteoarthritis, ageing is the main factor: it is a structural, degenerative disease without the auto-immune component found in other types of arthritis. Treatment is primarily for the pain, and total joint replacements are now commonplace and have excellent results, although, like all surgical procedures, they carry risks for older adults and pain, discomfort and inconvenience during and after hospitalization for the surgery.

A biological approach to the body does not, however, tell us everything about Alice's situation. From the short word-picture above, we can see that many aspects of her life are not captured by a purely biomedical perspective. For example, for many arthritis sufferers, the constant pain and the need to gain relief is the dominant impact of the disease. Traditionally, health care professionals have not been good at managing pain, as it is a subjective experience and cannot easily be assessed. People may under-report their pain, as they try to 'grin and bear it', or find strategies to manage pain by reducing their daily activity. Specialist pain clinics now provide a more patient-centred approach to pain management, and the emergence of powerful but non-addictive pain medications means that rheumatologists now have more tools to improve pain management.

Nor is biomedicine well suited to address the wider psychological and emotion impact of disability. The emphasis on pathology ignores the social impacts of loss of mobility or dependency. For Alice, living in her own house and sustaining independence is central to her social identity. She does not think of herself as a patient, or as a disabled elderly person, she is the same person she was when she was younger, and she has an investment in her life-story. Disease threatens her sense-of-self as much as it does her body, and the future offers only uncertainty and the prospect of a deteriorating capacity to 'be herself' independently of others or of the health professions. For Alice, her body is not just a thing she has, it is also who she is; part of her identity. She hates the way her body lets her down and may force her to ask more of her grown-up children in support.

Finally, the biological model of the body does not address the social and economic consequences of disease and illness. In the twenty-first century, many people will be working, pursuing leisure and other pursuits into their eighties and beyond. Alice can expect many years of life ahead, but her condition will limit her capacities to be socially and economically active. Poverty afflicts many older adults and social isolation is a major consequence of illness and disability. Alice has an active interest in the world around her and is active in the support group and collecting for an arthritis charity. But her condition will reduce her capacity to engage and old age may be a time of progressive loss of contact with the outside world, as both lack of mobility and lack of social and economic resources limit what she and her body can do.

In addition, Alice's body, her doctors and her carers are connected not just by pathology and the application of bio-medical knowledge to its treatment. The medical care of bodies takes place within a social, economic and political context that includes systems of health care provision, public and private providers and the medicinal products such as pharmaceuticals and devices that are produced commercially for profit. In some countries such as the UK, Alice Martin may have access to free care funded by taxation, while in others such as the US and Australia, private or public insurance schemes may fund her care. Which treatments are available may be constrained by costs, subject to rationing or influenced by political assessments of what can be afforded or what role the state should have in health care provision. New treatments may develop more because of their profitability than to meet need.

Try to draw out other aspects of Alice's body not encompassed by a biological model: I shall be returning to Alice as we explore other perspectives on the body. For now, I hope this case study has shown how the biological body provides some important understanding of embodiment, but fails to fully capture the richness of what it is to have, and to be, a body. Health professionals clearly need to understand the biological basis of the human body, as this underpins the physical and psychological aspects of health and illness. However, the case study suggests that they also need to recognize the wider contexts of embodiment. If they do not, they may fail to provide care that addresses the needs of the people they treat, or see merely a series of diseases paraded in front of them rather than people whose embodied lives are complex, rich and multi-faceted.

## Suggested further reading

Dennett, D. C. (1996) *Darwin's Dangerous Idea: Evolution and the Meanings of Life*. Harmondsworth: Penguin.

Porter, R. (2003) *Blood and Guts: A Short History of Medicine*. Harmondsworth: Penguin.

# CHAPTER TWO

# The Social Body

The last chapter explored the ways in which biological and medical sciences have developed the biomedical model of the body over the past 200 years, based on a scientific view of how structure relates to function. I showed how this model has become very well established in contemporary Western culture, to the extent that the biomedical body is often the 'common-sense' or lay version that many people refer to when thinking about embodiment and what a body is. The biological model extends into many aspects of lay 'body-talk', including sport and fitness, diet, physical appearance and body shape, and gender and sexuality. The biology of the body: everything from its surface anatomy to the organs and processes of digestion, circulation, reproduction, sensation and cognition, may be used as a reference point against which to assert values (of beauty, fitness, health or attractiveness), assess bodily performance or even to market a product to enhance the body in some way. As life in the West becomes more and more influenced by science, biomedicine continually extends its ability to define the body, normal and pathological.

The biological view of the body is not, however, the only perspective that people use to make sense of embodiment. The aim of this chapter is to begin to document other ways in which people and societies have addressed embodiment and how these approaches help to understand embodiment in health and social care. I will look at the social body, as it has been uncovered by research findings from sociology, psychology, anthropology, psychoanalysis and political philosophy and ethics. The chapter will introduce the main theoretical perspectives on the body in society, although the intention here is to provide an overview which can be built upon in later chapters when we look at specific aspects of embodiment. To illustrate these social approaches to the body, I will examine once again the case study of chronic illness introduced in chapter 1, to see what additional insights we can glean.

## Society, social science and the body

So what is the 'social body' and why is there a social body at all?

The answer to these questions rests with the capacity of human beings to interact with, and reflect upon, the world around them and, specifically, to interpret and attach meanings to objects they perceive in the environment. Through the medium of language, humans conceptualize the world they experience, and use these concepts to represent, categorize and differentiate elements of reality. Children learn the concepts used in their culture, and usually adopt the same categories and representations. Sometimes, as we gain experience, we may also develop our own concepts and categories, even when these diverge from those used by our contemporaries (Hart and McKinnon 2010: 1041). Invention, creativity and the innovation of ideas and technologies reflect this capacity to devise novel concepts and categories to explain the world, or even to create imaginary worlds independent of sensory input from the environment.

Despite this capacity for novelty and divergent imagining, much of the time humans share an interpretation of our environment with their fellows, to the extent that we are able to communicate and collaborate around these shared meanings (Hart and McKinnon 2010). However, these shared meanings (which in time establish a culture across a society or community) do not work at the level of the objects themselves, but through the concepts and the words we apply to these objects. This ability to establish shared concepts for objects in our environment has been called the 'social construction of reality'

(Berger and Luckmann 1991). This important idea means that everything: a table, a dog or a disease, is inevitably a socially constructed concept as well as being a 'real' object. We actually live out our lives not only in a world of the 'things themselves', but also within an array of concepts with specific cultural and social meanings (Hart and McKinnon 2010).

Human cultures thus have the capacity to establish consensus around interpretations and meanings. These social constructions are hugely useful on a day-to-day basis: they create regularity and predictability, smoothing off the sharp edges of an unpredictable reality with norms and expectations about how things are and how they behave. However, the social construction of reality through concepts can also create divisions between social groups (nations, communities, age groups, professions and so forth) with divergent constructions of reality. The struggle for power between political parties reflects humans' capacity to interpret the same facts in multiple ways, for example in the entirely different analyses of economic or social issues offered by the political Left and political Right. These differences may be quite critical: the world almost went to nuclear war over the rival conceptions of human progress held by those of capitalist and communist persuasions in the second half of the twentieth century. At a more mundane level, the proposition that 'men are from Mars and women are from Venus' suggests that males and females may not always see the world around them similarly. Try to think of other examples where a group or community understands their world differently from others.

This brings us back to the body. We all know a lot about bodies, because we all have one, and its structures and functions are of great importance to us on a minute-by-minute basis as we breathe, eat, reproduce, sleep and so forth. We experience our bodies directly via our senses, but as children develop language and the capacity to use concepts, the body also quickly gains a *social construction*. From the age of two or thereabouts, we begin to construct our own bodies socially, as we learn the meanings that our parents and other members of our culture hold about bodies and embodiment. (Of course, we possess socially constructed bodies from birth, even when in the womb: every culture attaches meanings to the bodies of the newborn and the unborn.) Our social bodies become more and more rich in meanings as we gain more experience of embodiment, for example in relation to physical fitness, sexual development and desire, and growth and ageing. This process continues throughout life: embodiment for a young person may mean opportunity and fulfilment, while for someone with a debilitating chronic or degenerative illness it may mean pain, mortality and dependency.

Throughout history, the body has been a rich source both of lay beliefs and a measure of things, both physical and metaphorical. People live through their bodies, so it is hardly surprising that the body is used as a cultural resource to shape the values and meanings that people use to organize their life. This has also meant that the body has been a focus for what the social philosopher Michel Foucault called 'discipline', by which he means the processes of educating, controlling and civilizing bodies, of which more later in this chapter. For the past 150 years, social scientists have also contributed their own economic, sociological, psychological and cultural analysis of the body and its significance (as have biological scientists).

The body thus has gained unrivalled richness in potential meanings. This has led inevitably to the importance of the body and embodiment in most human cultures, both for itself and as a marker or metaphor for other things, including social cohesion, group identity and social or economic position. These meanings will vary from culture to culture, and historically. Sometimes body concepts have associated negative attributes with the body, in other circumstances, embodiment has been conceived positively. More often, there remains ambivalence: embodiment can have both positive and negative attributes: even in today's Western culture, embodiment is socially constructed both as a great gift for personal fulfilment and human progress through work and ingenuity, and a source of weakness or temptation that must be disciplined in order to benefit both the individual and society.

As noted at the start of this chapter, the physical body is increasingly (but not exclusively) the province of a scientific, biomedical model. This model of the physical body superseded earlier perspectives on the body's form, in many of which moral evaluations of character or personality were associated with physical bodily characteristics. England's King Richard III, reviled for his evil behaviour and corruption in the centuries following his defeat in battle by his rival Henry Tudor (the future Henry VII), was often portrayed artistically as a crippled hunchback, though there is no independent evidence of him having such a disability. The painter William Hogarth showed the poor, dissolute and criminal as ugly and disfigured in his visual essays on English urban depravity, as were people with learning disabilities or mental health problems in later (pseudo)scientific representations. Even in the twentieth century, physical impairments had negative connotations: a visually impaired person might be assumed to be deaf (a helper is asked: 'does he take sugar?'), deaf people to have a learning disability, and learning-disabled people to have deviant sexual appetites.

To a modern eye, these earlier associations may seem outlandish, prejudiced and even cruel. Cultural beliefs about deviations from bodily norms reflected pre-scientific efforts to make sense of such divergences: with divine punishment or immorality offered as the reason for deformity, disability or infirmity. Modern biomedicine has swept aside some of these prejudices, and the neutrality of biomedicine has released many people from the 'stigma' (a mark or blemish) of a physical divergence from a norm of bodily appearance or of fitness (Goffman 1970). Some prejudices remain: obesity is becoming a new stigmatizing condition in a world in which slimness and under-nourishment are associated with glamour and beauty, and over-indulgence an indicator of environmental irresponsibility or moral weakness (Gard and Wright 2005: 7).

The reason that such associations were made and continue to be made is not, however, simply because of ignorance or fear. It is because the body is more than just the collection of physical organs, cells, molecules or processes that biology teaches. For thousands of years, the body has been a potent and important element in how people understand and socially construct themselves as human actors. The body is both the physicality of a biological organism, *and* a key element in the social construction of human culture and human identity. For health care professionals, this means that the body cannot be reduced to its biological make-up. Just as important is the social body, which is constructed from the cultural concepts of a society and individual experiences and sensations, and is also a key element in constituting other aspects of personhood, including identity, perspective on life and responses to illness and to care.

Social scientists have variously recognized that the social body is an important subject for their study, in parallel with the studies and developing understanding of biological scientists. The body, now more than ever, is the focus for the social sciences, which seek to explain and understand the social processes that surround and indeed construct the body. Medical anthropologists Scheper-Hughes and Lock (1987) identified three social aspects of the body: a body that serves as a metaphor or symbol for other things; a 'body-politic' that is regulated and controlled by society; and a 'lived body' of experience. In the remainder of this chapter, I shall look at these social aspects of the body and the various ways in which social science has offered insights and tools to make sense of embodiment.

## Bodies, symbols and rituals

In the introduction to the book, I discussed how artistic representations of the body illustrate how an artist and her/his contemporary viewers understood embodiment. The study of cultural artefacts such as paintings, sculpture or other representations of the body can tell us how a society considered the human body and how these beliefs, attitudes and values have changed. The human form, for example, has been represented quite differently in different periods or cultures, from the emphasis on symmetry and perfection in studies of ancient Greek athletes or warriors, through the imperfect sinful bodies of medieval Christian art and the tragic bodies of Romantic artists' portrayal of poverty and social injustice, to the eroticization of the body in Hindu religious icons, Victorian art and contemporary soft porn.

However, the physical body may not only be an object to be represented artistically, but also a marker of something other than itself. The body can be a 'carrier' for culture, by means of marks or modification, ranging from minor, temporary changes such as a hair style, cosmetics or piercings, to extreme and permanent marks including tattoos, scarification or surgery and mutilation. Bodies and their constituent parts (limbs, hair, genitals etc.), because of the richness of their associated meanings, are also ideal substrates for symbolism: the capacity of one thing to represent or stand for another, usually in order to justify some position or argument concerning the organization of society or a group (Douglas 1996: 69).

The cultural sociologist Anthony Synnott has documented some of the symbolism of the body in Western culture. In ancient Greece, the philosophers Plato and Socrates considered the body as a 'tomb' in which the soul was trapped; only by death could it be freed from its bodily prison (Synnott 1993: 9). While the body was also a source of sin and ungodliness for Christians, it was also described by St Paul (the architect of much of Christianity's doctrine) as a temple by which humans could demonstrate their divine origin through righteousness (ibid.: 14). Synnott suggests that the body and the face are now symbols of selfhood (ibid.: 2, 73), while hair (and how it is styled) can symbolize group identity (ibid.: 103), as monks and punks, hippies and skinheads have all grasped. Each of these symbols uses the body to make a different point; usually about how to live or behave, or about the wider society or sub-culture. Body parts also carry symbolic meanings. Think of the heart: not just a pump for blood, but also a symbol of love, emotional responses in general and also integrity or moral strength. Feeling 'jaundiced' can mean not only suffering a liver pathology but also being disillusioned with life or love!

In her anthropological analyses of Western and non-Western societies, Mary Douglas found that body symbols have been used to represent three different aspects of social organization. First, symbols of how a body's organs or limbs relate to the whole can represent the relationship between a monarch, leader or state and the citizenry. Second, failure to control diet or avoid bodily excretions can represent the risks faced by a society, for example from migration or enemy spies. Finally, the body may represent a society that is sick or dysfunctional: freedom from this social sickness can be achieved only by rejecting the body altogether (Douglas 1996: xxxvi).

Body symbols that represent (and enhance) social relations are often manifested in rituals and ceremonies. Bodies and their display or movements play an important role in many rituals and are often invested with specific clothing or uniforms, badges or ornamentations and other adornments such as temporary or permanent bodily marks. The white dress and veil mark the symbolic sexual purity of a bride on her wedding day; crowning confirms the rights of monarchy; while gowns and caps mark the transition from undergraduate to graduate status at a university degree ceremony. These rites of transition (*rites de passage*) may also require bodily movement through space: traditionally a bride is accompanied up the church aisle by her father or other male relative, stands or kneels before a priest and then, in her new married status, departs with her husband. A graduation ceremony is marked by processions and handshakes between graduating students and the senior official of the university. These movements symbolize the attainment of the new status or authority (van Gennep 2004).

The use of the body or its elements to represent social organization continues in the contemporary rise in body adornment and fashions, hair styles and colouring, and tattoos and other marks, and concerns to achieve culturally defined norms of body shape. People choose to mark their allegiances to social groupings and classes through such symbolism, linking bodily symbols and body rituals to the wider concerns in society. Douglas believes that pretty much every aspect of embodiment reflects some aspect of social organization:

> ... the body itself is a highly restricted medium of expression. The forms it adopts in movement and repose express social pressures in manifold ways. The care that is given to it, in grooming, feeding and therapy, the theories about what it needs in the way of sleep and exercise, about the stages it should go through, the pains it can stand, its span of life, all the cultural categories in which it is perceived, must correlate closely with the categories in which society is seen, in so far as these also draw upon the same culturally processed idea of the body. (Douglas 1996: 69)

In some ways, this view of the body is the precise opposite of the biological model, but with the determinism of genes and physiology in biomedicine replaced by an equally determining social structure.

## The socialized and civilized body

Seeing the body as a resource for social symbolism and ritual inevitably opposes the 'natural' body and the cultural and social structures that impinge on this natural entity. This dualism is a theme that runs through many of the social theories of embodiment, including the idea of 'socialization'. Socialization addresses the ways in which a natural body (the body of biology that we encountered in chapter 1) can be 'civilized' by social forces; shaping it to fit the norms of society (for example, in terms of sexual behaviour, 'table manners' and respect for authority) and no longer prone to the impulses, emotions and desires that reflect humanity's animal origins (Elias 1991: 104).

According to psychologists, socialization is a process that begins shortly after birth, as the human infant is trained by rewards and punishments, play and mimicry, and eventually by rational persuasion, to adopt the norms of its culture in terms of physical behaviour, emotional display and control, sexuality and gender roles, language and accent, dietary preferences and other aspects of embodiment (Parsons and Bales 1956; Rutter 1985). The acquisition of a native language opens the child to the oral and written culture of her/his society, while schooling and subsequent education may be understood as further socialization into the knowledge, culture and values of a society.

From such a view, the embodied actions of a human are a consequence of how they have been socialized: little remains of the natural body other than the needs for air, water, food, and social and sexual interaction. Gender differences in embodied behaviour and roles, for example, may be wholly explained by the different socialization of boys and girls from the moment the boy is given a blue bib and a toy tractor and the girl a pink hat and a doll. The sociologist Erving Goffman argued that people must learn how to present themselves successfully to the world, in part through their bodily deportment (Goffman 1990). In a famous series of 'experiments with trust', another sociologist Harold Garfinkel (1967) found strong negative reactions towards people who broke the unspoken codes of behaviour that exist both in public and between friends and family. He concluded that humans must continually work on this presentation in order for the social order to hold together. Turner called this mastery of bodily techniques and practices 'doing a body' (Turner 1992: 40).

Sociologists and historians have taken this analysis a step further: not only is there a socialization during childhood, but over a historical time period, there has been a general tendency towards the 'civilization' of bodies. The cultural sociologist Norbert Elias (2000) argued in *The Civilising Process* that bodily functions have been progressively civilized: taking functions of the body such as eating, excretion and reproduction, and establishing codes of manners and propriety in how humans should behave in these aspects of embodiment. Building on this work, Mennell (1991) showed how appetite for foodstuffs varied over time and between social classes, while Foucault's *History of Sexuality* described different societal models and norms of civilized sexuality. Thus (remarkably from a modern standpoint) paedophilia was acceptable and encouraged in ancient Greece, while sexual control within marriage was an ideal for upper-class Romans, and abstinence encouraged in Christianity (Foucault 1984, 1985, 1986). The nineteenth-century sociologist Max Weber argued that the work ethic (the celebration of abstinence and hard work over pleasure and idleness), the emergence of ideas of professionalism and work as a 'calling' or vocation, and even the economic system of capitalism were all grounded in Protestant Christianity's rejection of the body and its urges (Weber 1971: 155).

For these writers, something as apparently 'natural' as appetite or sexuality turns out to be a product of culture: the body is progressively trained and constrained by social norms. Foucault's take on this led him to a general view of the body as the focus for social control and discipline (Foucault 1980). I will consider this perspective in more detail in chapter 6, when I focus on the management of bodies, but you may like to think now about how your body and daily bodily activities may be constrained and shaped by cultural norms, expectations and values.

One of the earliest thinkers concerning the socialization of the body was the Victorian psychiatrist Sigmund Freud. Freud introduced a radical conception of the human body, suggesting that humans are born with animal drives or desires that seek to satiate the bodily needs for food, security and sexual satisfaction. Infants are entirely selfish, with all their energy devoted to satisfying bodily needs. But from birth onwards, humans are progressively trained to subjugate these body desires, with the result that a 'civilized' being emerges as children learn to control their desires. Adulthood marks the emergence of a fully socialized personality that no longer selfishly pursues food or sexual gratification. Instead, adults pursue work, artistic or scientific endeavours or charity: features of the civilized society that Freud observed around him (Freud 1973: 216).

However, Freud argued that the innate desires of the child are not obliterated by the socialization process. Rather, they are suppressed or repressed, with possible negative consequences, both for the individual and for society. The conscious, rational self or 'ego' keeps control of the unconscious desires of the 'id', while the values and norms of society are internalized to serve as a kind of body police (the 'superego'), to prevent the selfish desires of the id to surface. Mental health problems such as neurosis and psychosomatic symptoms, Freud argued, were manifestations of this internal conflict between these three components of the personality. His therapeutic remedy, psychoanalysis, was a means to address the conflict: once a patient realized her or his body had repressed desires, this insight allowed the conflict to be resolved. Freud also argued that the great achievements of civilized society (democracy, art, science and so forth) were not simply the products of human rationality, but the consequence of the repression of bodily desires which emerge unconsciously in acts of heroism, creativity or altruism (Freud 1957).

For today's unbuttoned society, Freud's insight is almost part of the psychic landscape, and we are now encouraged to allow a freer rein to our body desires and their gratification. When Freud was writing, his ideas were more disturbing to society, as they suggested that in all of us – beneath the veneer of civilization – lurked a selfish, animal id, only partially repressed and always threatening to break through to reveal the body's unconscious desires. Contemporary literary manifestations of the dark side of human nature included Mr Hyde, the *alter ego* of the respectable Dr Jekyll in Robert Louis Stevenson's 1886 novel, and Bram Stoker's *Dracula*, published in 1897. The twentieth century embraced Freudianism, although now more as a cultural model of embodiment and society than as an effective therapy for mental health problems. Freud's legacy is principally to expose the conflicts between the body as a desiring, biological entity and the constraints that society imposes on how bodies are to be managed and constrained. Psychoanalytic approaches have been influential in social models of the body, particularly within feminism (for example, Cixous 1986; Kristeva 1986), and as the starting point for a theory of desire as a positive force (Deleuze and Guattari 1984). Desire will be explored more fully in chapter 5.

## Time and the working body

One of the ways in which the body is socialized is through the routine of the working day (Adam 1990; Zerubavel 1979). For workers, school students and consumers, the industrial revolution brought into being a daily rhythm that was governed by the clock. Whereas an agrarian society was dominated by the daily cycle of sunrise and sunset, the emergence of a factory system in the eighteenth and nineteenth centuries established a working day of fixed length, with 'clocking-on' and 'clocking-off' times at the start and finish of each shift. Sirens and bells now created a routine to the day, demarcating work or school attendance from leisure time. Workers' lives fitted round the need for the factory to sustain production, rather than production meeting human needs. Over the next one hundred years, opening hours for shops, pubs and banks were also progressively regulated, establishing patterns to the working week, mealtimes and holidays, with an obligatory weekly day of rest on the Sabbath.

One consequence of this was that workers could now be paid by the hour, rather than by the job. The relationship between the effort expended by bodies during work and the financial reward became transparent, as did the different rates of pay for different work. The political and economic writings of the nineteenth-century radical social theorist and econo-mist Karl Marx cast another angle on the socialized body. Marx was concerned to understand and critically evaluate the workings of industrial capitalism, in which capital (money, resources) were invested in manufacturing enterprises with the prime objective of generating profit. Profit was the differ-ence between what it cost to make a product and the amount for which it could be sold in the market. Marx discovered the source of this profit: the work carried out by human bodies that enabled the value of goods to be enhanced during the industrial process (Marx 1951).

To illustrate this, let's imagine what's involved in manufac-turing a mobile phone, a motor car or a surgical instrument. The employer has three main costs. First, there are the raw materials (metals, plastics and so forth). Second, there will be overheads (the cost of the factory, electricity to run the machinery, bank loan interest and so on). Finally, there will be a wage bill, to pay the workforce to make the product. From the point of view of this book, the latter is the most interest-ing of these costs. Marx concluded that there is an exchange here between the employee and the employer: a worker effec-tively sells her or his *labour power* (the capacity to undertake physical or mental work) to the employer in return for a wage. Employers would purchase the necessary numbers of hours, days and weeks from workers in order to undertake the work needed to turn raw materials into a finished product (ibid.). More highly skilled workers can demand a higher wage, because their labour power is greater and will transform raw materials into more valuable goods for a given amount of input.

Thus, to pursue the example of mobile phone manufac-ture, the less skilled work of assembling the phones adds less value to the finished product than the design of the circuitry, the writing and development of software, and the product branding and marketing, all of which may involve a graduate workforce. The latter staff can sell their labour power for more than the unskilled labour and will receive a higher wage. Training can augment skills and thus will enable workers to enhance the wages they can demand for a job of work. However, skilled or unskilled, the worker must sell her/his labour power continually in order to gain the wages to live.

The relevance of Marx's analysis to embodiment is clear: labour power is an attribute of the physical body (including the brain): human bodies are needed, in order to provide the labour power to transform raw materials into cars and phones and surgical instruments, products with added value, in order for a profit to be achieved. Employers must try to minimize the costs of purchasing labour power, in order to maximize their profits. During the last century, industrial manufacturing processes have become much more sophisticated. Tools, from the chisels used by a wood turner to a loom for weaving cloth, have been superseded by industrial robots that can turn out cars or phones on a production line without human intervention, enhance productivity, enabling more units of goods to be produced in a given time. But these robots were themselves designed, developed and built by highly skilled human bodies in the first place; so again, it was bodily work that delivered the increases in production.

Marx criticized capitalism for turning the capacities of human bodies into a commodity, to be bought and sold. The industrial process transforms a body's labour power into cars and phones and other goods and services that are produced and eventually sold for a profit. He considered this a dehumanizing process, which reduced humans to elements in a drive to secure a profit from a capital investment. He argued for an alternative economic system (communism), which would enable labour power to be used for the good of society and human advancement rather than simply to turn a profit for the owners of capital (Marx and Engels 2009). Marx's analysis thus provides a perspective on the body that is economic, political and sociological, yet recognizes the biological body as the source of creativity and production. His work holds in tension the biological and the social, in a way that some other theories of embodiment do not.

Marx's notion of labour power has some similarity to that of 'physical capital', employed by the sociologist Bourdieu to explain how people engage with the world around them: in work, leisure and other social aspects of daily life (Shilling 1991: 654–6), and also the continuity of class and other inequalities in societies. In Bourdieu's view, physical capital is a resource that can be replenished and augmented by exploiting social judgements about the value of certain bodily competencies (for instance, sporting excellence, the photogenic body or face of a model, or the manual dexterity of a surgeon), and can be converted into other types of capital (including financial) to enhance social advantage and position. Shilling (1991) argues that variations between men's and women's opportunities to exploit their physical capital, and differences in the value placed on physical competencies (domestic caring work, for example, is not valued highly in Western society), may help to explain gender inequalities.

## Feminism and the gendered body

Perhaps in response to the widespread patriarchal view in the earlier part of the twentieth century that women reflected the 'natural', while men represented the rational and cultural aspect of humanity (Butler 1990: x; Shildrick 1996: 1), feminist scholars have developed a well-rounded analysis of the social construction of gender and sexuality (Witz 2000: 1). Part of this sought to oppose and reject a dominant biological and biomedical view of the female body, which contributed to a general oppression of women, specifically but not exclusively concerning reproduction and sexuality (Darke 1996: 144–7; Graham 1979; Oakley 1980: 10). These critics argue that women's bodies have become objectified, and women's subjectivity ignored or denied. Biomedicine, in part, serves as an obstacle to women taking control of their own embodiment and their very selves (Boston Women's Health Collective 1978). Thus, for example, Graham and Oakley (1986) showed how childbirth had become medicalized, with women's wishes concerning the birth ignored or marginalized. Darke (1996) discusses the role of hormone replacement therapy (HRT) in medicalizing the menopause.

These studies, informed by feminism and radical sexual politics, have established an important critical legacy concerning embodiment: the recognition that gender plays a critical role both in how embodiment is experienced, and in the way that society and culture construct gendered bodies and replicate these gender differences over time. The early criticisms of modern society as patriarchal, and of biomedicine as a source of power over women, have been augmented with many studies that demonstrate the continuing discourses that establish gendered bodies. In a study of female embodiment in the workplace, Brewis (2000) found that the physical appearance of the body was a marker of their age, status and rank within their work organization, and that women struggled to overcome stereotypes and prejudice, for instance of motherhood. The preference in Western cultures for slim female bodies serves both to discipline women's diets, and to create guilt when they fall short of the slim ideal (Featherstone 1991: 177; Fox et al. 2005a, b). Cultural concepts of embodiment concerning gender and sexuality do not only affect women's bodies. In our consumer culture, the emergence of effective treatments for male impotence and male pattern baldness have both led to a medicalization and 'pharmaceuticalization' of male bodies (Fox and Ward 2008a), as ideals of youth and physical fitness also influence male embodiment and identities (Featherstone and Hepworth 1982).

Recent feminist studies of embodiment have re-introduced an interest in the dual character of the body as both biological and social, and its consequence for identity. Butler (1990) makes the case that gender emerges out of social interactions ('performances') and that there is no underlying female (or male) gender identity. Hird (2000: 348) notes that female and male genders are measured against an assumed standard of male and female biological 'sex', yet recent research evidence suggests that a dualistic concept of biological sex is an over-simplification that gives apparent validity to gender differences that are actually more to do with social norms and patriarchal social organization. Shildrick (1996) and Haraway (1991) invite us to celebrate a gendered body that has the capacity to disrupt and challenge norms. For these writers, the female body is a source of identity and empowerment.

Later in this book I will devote further space to these ideas, in a further exploration of gender, sexuality and embodiment, focusing on the interaction between the biological and social aspects of embodied sexuality and desire.

## The lived body

So far I have looked at a number of perspectives based upon the idea that a body is something that one 'has'. This body, according to these views, turns out not just to be a biological entity, but something constrained and controlled by social forces: from Marx's economics and politics of production, through to the civilizing effects of culture on how bodies are required to behave.

Much of the recent work on the body and embodiment has argued that this idea of the body has to be augmented with an understanding of the body as something that one 'is'. In other words, we have to look at the experience of living with a body, and through a body. Sociologists have focused on this dual aspect of embodiment, which recognizes the body not only as a thing that interacts with society, but also as the medium by which we are able to live our lives, and establish and sustain an individual, reflexive (capable of self-reflection) identity

(Turner 1992: 40). They have suggested that it is this duality that makes embodiment such a key factor in many aspects of life, from illness behaviour, to gender and sexual identity, to development and ageing. The sociologist Bryan Turner offers an example of how this dual perspective affects the study of embodiment: we may be interested not only in the effect of gender on embodiment (for instance, in role socialization or the bodily consequences of reproductive capability), but also on 'what it is like to be a woman (or a man)' (ibid.: 41). He argues that this kind of question is particularly important in the study of embodiment and health, as it encourages us to focus on the embodied experience of health and illness from a patient perspective, and the impact of illness, pain and disability upon identity (ibid.: 157–8).

We can summarize this perspective as 'the lived body', recognizing the narrative of embodied experience and interpretation that each of us lives through from our first moments of consciousness in infancy to our last. The philosopher Maurice Merleau-Ponty emphasized the importance of the body as the means of perceiving the world around us (Merleau-Ponty 2002: 380). Indeed, he argued, 'in order to perceive things, we need to live them' (ibid.: 379). The lived body is also reflexive; it can 'turn back upon itself, to experience itself' (Crossley 1995: 49). Embodied experience interacts with its social context, and the lived body both produces and is produced by this context (Nettleton and Watson 1998: 11).

Various areas of the lived body have been explored in recent sociological studies. Emotions ('felt thoughts'): those peculiarly internal experiences that can have strong physical effects (from flushes and blushes to nausea or paralysing fear) and which appear to be entirely 'natural', biological responses to circumstances, actually link the most innermost experiences of the embodied self to the wider social contexts of the world around us. Hochschild (1979) found class differences between how people are trained or socialized to manage their emotions, while Duncombe and Marsden (1993) argued that the differences between men and women were down to different socialization, with an emotional division of labour within households, in which women took responsibility for the emotional aspects of family life. 'Emotion work' may be an important part of the caring role of health professionals, providing support to patients who are vulnerable and frightened by their illness (James 1989; Kleinman 1988). Williams and Bendelow (1998a: 154) conclude that emotions play an important role in determining whether the social world is perceived as conducive or alienating, thus influencing the continuity or change within societies.

Pain, another seemingly personal and individual experience, can also be explored from the perspective of the lived body. The body, often unnoticed in everyday life, can suddenly make its presence known and felt when pain impinges upon it (Williams and Bendelow 1998a: 159). This is particularly relevant for our case study of chronic illness. In a book of reflections on the lived body, Kleinman (1988) looked at how pain is experienced in chronic illness, and how people construct narratives to make sense of their experiences.

> The illness narrative is a story the patient tells . . . to give coherence to the distinctive events and long term course of suffering. Over the long course of chronic disorder, these model texts shape and even create experience. The personal narrative does not merely reflect illness experience, but . . . contributes to the experience of symptoms and suffering. (Kleinman 1988: 49)

Pain is an individual experience and one that cannot easily be described in language. People make sense of their suffering by reflection and giving meaning to their pain (Williams and Bendelow 1998b: 139). It follows that the lived body is a rich source of meaning for people, in sickness and in health: people make sense of their lives by reflecting on their bodily experience. I will conclude this chapter by looking again at the case study of chronic illness, to illustrate some of the themes that have emerged around the social body.

## Conclusions: challenging biological determinism

The perspectives presented in this chapter offer a very different angle on the character of embodiment from that provided by the biological models set out in chapter 1. To consider what has been added to an understanding of the body, let us look again at the case study of chronic illness we first encountered in chapter 1. You will recall Alice Martin, a 75-year-old widow who suffers from osteoarthritis, which is treated with medications, a knee replacement and two planned hip replacements. We saw how arthritis has become part of Alice's life, affecting many of her activities including walking, cooking and driving a car. She fears she will eventually be house-bound, or have to move into supported housing, losing some independence. She is active in the local Arthritis Support Group, as well as an arthritis charity.

I noted in the last chapter that the biomedical approach to the body is good at describing the relationship between degeneration and function, but inadequate to explore the experiential side of Alice's chronic illness, or to describe the suffering associated with illness (Morris 2000: 193). This chapter on the social body now allows us to flesh out these aspects. A social perspective begins by recognizing that while bodies, health and illness may be grounded in biology, our experiences of these biological realities are refracted through the lens of the social, psychological and economic context. Human beings are reflexive about the world that they experience, including their own bodies. They make sense of their experiences in terms of what they already know, the norms and values of their culture, and through making links between experiences and ideas and concepts.

One of the most important aspects of chronic illness emerges from this. Illness is never 'just' illness: it has specific meaning for the person and as such will be unique to them. Alice has fears for the future, about her independence, her economic security and her well-being as she grows older. Fear is a common element in the experience of chronic illness, as the future is uncertain and may represent a threat to many of the things a person has established in their lifetime and holds dear (Fox 2005). Similarly, pain can have particularly profound meanings for the ill: pain is a subjective experience but its meaning is also socially contextual. There is a difference between the pain resulting from a minor accident; falling off a bike for example, and the pain that lasts day-in, day-out as a consequence of a degenerative or systemic disease. The difference lies not in the physical sensation but in the recognition that the latter will not go away, and that it is a result not of trauma but of an underlying pathology which may progress in the future.

This chapter touched on some other aspects of the social body that are relevant to Alice's illness. If the body stands as a symbol of social order, then illness may represent the decay or corruption of that order. Healthy bodies are usually also civilized bodies, while the dependency that comes with illness may lead to a loss of dignity, as the body no longer performs to the standards its owner desires. Even dressing oneself or using the toilet can be a problem for those with debilitating illness. Marx's analysis of bodies and capitalism means that Alice has little labour power to sell: illness can be a time of poverty as a consequence. With poverty comes social isolation: a further blow for those who have already lost a spouse.

Finally, the analysis of the social body begins to make crucial links between embodiment and identity. A biological model of illness struggles to grasp that the body and its functions are a source of identity. We carry our identity with us through life, using our experiences to provide a sense of a continuing self, and bolstering those aspects of ourselves that provide integration and a well-rounded identity. Like the rest of us, Alice has established a sense of who she is over her life, living in her own house, looking after herself, and making her way in the world economically and socially; these all contribute to her social identity. With dependency can come a challenge to this: losing the independence that comes with a walk to the shops or a visit to the theatre can be a devastating blow (Fox and Ward 2008b). Although her doctor has defined her as such because of the osteoarthritis, Alice does not think of herself primarily as a patient, or as a disabled elderly person. Rather she is herself: a mother, a worker, and a member of a range of social networks. But the health care system can challenge these identities, replacing them with the master-identity of patient (Charmaz 1995), and forcing Alice to adapt. Charmaz suggests that as chronically ill people accommodate to bodily losses and limits, they revise their identity goals and 'surrender to the sick self by relinquishing control over illness' (ibid.: 657).

In this chapter we have recognized the 'parallel' social body that contextualizes the biological body. It would be wrong, however, to conclude that this social body somehow is superimposed on the 'real' biology of the body. Rather, it is better to think of biology and the social world as together constituting embodiment. For health professionals, biological and social factors both contribute important aspects of the bodies of their patients. The challenge they face is to keep both elements in play, not privileging one over the other. James (1989) argued that the social and emotional care that health professionals provide is as important as the work they do on biological bodies. Yet it can be the first element of care to be abandoned when the pressure is on. By contrast, care that ignores the biological is potentially unethical and can limit the effectiveness of therapy.

Biological and social theorists of the body are both guilty of reducing the body to their preferred register. In the next chapter I shall outline the approach I shall use throughout the rest of the book, to ensure that biology and the social are both acknowledged as essential relations in human embodiment.

## Suggested further reading

Elias, N. (2000) *The Civilizing Process*. Oxford: Blackwell.

Shilling, C. (1991) Educating the body: physical capital and the production of social inequalities. *Sociology*, 25, 653–72.

Witz, A. (2000) Whose body matters? Feminist sociology and the corporeal turn in sociology and feminism. *Body and Society*, 6 (2), 1–24.

# CHAPTER THREE

# What Can a Body Do?

I have offered an overview in the previous chapters of how the biological and social sciences have described and sought to explain the human body. There is no end in sight to the capacity of researchers in these two different areas of science to generate more and more detail about bodies, yet there are few points of contact between the natural and the social bodies that this research has documented and indeed created.

For some, this is not a problem. For the biologist and the social scientist in their university departments, there is no great need to engage with their counterparts, or to do other than to acknowledge the other realm, and then swiftly turn back to their favoured perspective. We have seen how biological science has made inroads into the realm of the social, to explain behaviour and social organization in terms of evolutionary theory. Meanwhile, social scientists have ignored the physicality of the body until recently, regarding biology as irrelevant to the structures and processes of human societies, cultures and economies. Where it is acknowledged, it is often seen merely as a substrate for how the social world then moulds the body.

A focus on either the biological or the social body, however, is not an option for those whose daily work concerns bodies, health and social care professionals among them. For people who engage throughout their working day with the embodied realities of others' lives (from the experience of pain or the progression of disease, to the impact of illness or disability on relationships, finances or ability to live independently), we cannot simply pigeonhole the body into one or other category. The body is *both* a natural organism and a social entity. The bodies of patients and their carers inevitably exist within both the biological and social realms, although one or other can easily be privileged over the other. Medical students are taught about the social and psychological contexts of their patients' lives, yet medical education is still dominated by the biological sciences. The nursing theorist Veronica James noted (1989) that while emotional work with patients is critical to good nursing practice, it is all too easy for the demands to care for the physical body to overwhelm a nurse under pressure, with the loss of the human interactions with the 'social' bodies of his/her patients. Conversely, for a health or social care professional to overlook the physical needs or comfort of a vulnerable patient or client such as a child or elderly person, to focus on psychology or economic or social circumstances, would be unprofessional and have potentially fatal consequences. It is important for a health professional to understand the experience of illness, but alongside, rather than at the expense of, competence and capacity to treat disease.

For body theorists working to develop a coherent and holistic understanding of embodiment, it is important to find a way to explain the dual character of the body, without reducing one or other aspect to a footnote. If we can find a way to recognize that the body is always both biological and social, and that these aspects of its character together make it what it is, this can enhance the intellectual quality of our analysis, and consequently supply a coherent and effective blueprint for the body work of the health and social care professional, and the experiences of health, illness and care of their patients and clients.

As we have seen, the biologist and the social scientist start from different places (these days, at the molecular level for the former and at the cultural or even political level for the latter). They will tend to end up with explanations that reflect these starting points. Few academics or professionals have sufficient knowledge and experience of both traditions to move seamlessly between natural and social aspects of embodiment, nor should this be an essential requirement for a holistic insight. The aim of this chapter, then, is to find an approach that can encompass the biological and physical aspects of embodiment on one hand, and the social and cultural on the other, and be comprehensible to both natural and social science traditions. To do so, I shall offer a perspective that we have not yet encountered in this book, but which begins with the very simple question that is the title of this chapter: what can a body do?

## An ecology of the body

If we accept that the human body is both biological (an organism that is constituted from the physical constituents of atoms, molecules and cells), *and* social (an agent that engages with human culture and shapes that culture); if we take this as given, then it follows that the body has relations (to other things or people) in both these realms. A body will have relations through its organs and its senses with the physical world: the biological body eats, sleeps, breathes, reproduces, gets sick, dies, as a consequence of its physical relations with food, air, other bodies, microbes and so forth. But a body will also have relationships that are non-material, based on the social and psychological aspects of embodiment that we looked at in chapter 2. A body may also reflect upon its own physicality and shape an identity or sense-of-self that defines the body as young, old, healthy, sick, disabled and so on.

These relations (physical, social, psychological, emotional, political and so forth) both affect the body, and also how the body can influence or affect other entities. We could consider the sum of all these various relations and influences that a body has as its 'ecology': the body in its material and social context or environment. To develop this, let us now look in more detail at some of the relations a body can have, using the case study of Alice Martin encountered earlier in the book.

*Material relations*

Alice's physical body has direct relations with its material environment: it breathes in air and, as part of its respiratory and metabolic processes, uses oxygen to generate energy, in the process creating carbon dioxide, which is then expired. It also has relations to water and foodstuffs – plants, animals and other essential minerals, and passes the waste products of metabolism back into the environment. Through these processes the body grows from a single fertilized cell to a fully grown organism. More basically, the body has a relation to gravity, which both constrains it and permits it to function in specific ways. Alice's body is subject to injury and to attacks from chemicals, sunlight and infectious agents; it is also prone to degeneration over time, in her case leading to osteoarthritis. Through her senses (vision, hearing, touch etc.), Alice can apprehend the physical environment around it, including other bodies. Alice's body has also, during her lifetime, affected the environment and other bodies physically, directly or through the use of tools, in creative or destructive actions; through sexual contact and child-rearing; or in the many other daily interactions a body can have with what is around it.

*Psychological and emotional relations*

While the nervous impulses that pass information to and from the brain are part of the body's physical structures, Alice's cognitive capacities (its ability to process information or 'think') cannot be entirely reduced to biology. Cognitively and emotionally, humans and their interactions with the world are more complex than a 'black box' into which sensory stimuli (pleasurable or painful) may be fed, and out of which predictable responses emerge. Early in life, humans acquire a self-awareness and ability for self-reflection. These affect how the brain processes information, while memory and learning also influence how humans assess information and make complex decisions. Humans are also able to communicate with other sentient organisms, both through language and non-linguistically ('body-language'). This adds a further richness of relations that Alice's body can have, yet because communication can be misunderstood, it also adds uncertainty to her relations.

This capacity to filter, process and interpret incoming information using language and concepts, and decide on an appropriate response is the basis of 'thought'. So Alice's relations with the environment are mediated by this psychological capacity to think, reflect upon and process information. Her behaviour is similarly filtered through thought, language and concepts: Alice will choose to act not according to some kind of built-in response to a stimulus, but based on her reflections and judgements about the world and herself. Alice's response to pain, to a harsh word, or to a sunset reflect the *meanings* these events have for her.

In addition to cognitive processing, Alice's body will also respond emotionally to incoming information, while her emotional responses in turn affect others. Emotions: those strange amalgams of biology and the social, can have profound physical effects that can feel like a kick in the stomach or a starburst over our heads. Yet these apparently biological responses to events may be mediated by social norms and by experience and learning (a blush may be a response to a culturally defined embarrassment, such as nakedness in front of a stranger), so that emotions can be managed or even repressed. Think about your own emotional responses and how these may be influenced by norms or past experiences.

*Social and cultural relations*
Bodies relate to other humans, animals, even inanimate objects in ways that are more than simply physical: they love, or hate, or admire, or they care for these others; they engage and interact to build relationships that are intellectual and emotional, economic and political. The human capacity to interpret the world, and to communicate their interpretations of themselves, is the basis for human 'culture'.

In our everyday lives, every one of our bodies is deeply embedded in human culture: social institutions such as education or the workplace; wider political and economic systems; and the social and cultural groups to which we belong (from a group of friends through to a nation). Human culture may create religious or philosophical relations with ideas and ideals; philosophical or political creeds; divinities that define good and bad; and rules about how one 'should' behave, and what should happen if these rules are transgressed. Our bodies sustain and strengthen or weaken these cultural and social constructions through their daily relations with other bodies, institutions and ideas: we are all shaping human culture as we live out our lives.

Alice's body contributes to making this social world of interactions, beliefs, norms and values in all her relations with other bodies, every day of her life. As we saw in chapter 2, bodies or body parts may have symbolic meanings for individuals and groups; they may serve as the vehicle to communicate ideas, beliefs, or to mark the possessor of the body as a member of some grouping, class, gender or ethnic division; they may possess physical capital (beauty, physical prowess) that can be used to gain resources or advantage. Alice's body has social relations that may affect other bodies in all these ways. Her illness creates relations with health professionals based on her role as a 'patient'; she has social relations as mother or grandmother, a friend or a neighbour; she is an abstract 'citizen' in a society structured by age, class and gender.

So Alice's body (and all our bodies) may have all of these different, two-way relations with its physical and social context. This is the *ecology* of the body, as it engages with its environment. Each individual body has different relations, contingent upon its particular circumstances. A child's relations will usually be less complex than an adult's: memory and learning influence a person's relations. An occupation may affect relations: for a politician, a lawyer or a doctor, the relationship with another body will be affected (in both directions) by their responsibilities and the knowledge they possess. Non-human bodies also have relations. A blackbird has vocal cords (and neural pathways) that can form a relation with air. It has a relation to the dawning day and to predators in its environment that will affect how it will behave. And the singing blackbird has a multitude of social relations with other bodies (blackbirds and other animals) concerning mating, or warning, or marking territory (Deleuze and Guattari 1988: 312). For an insect, once again the relations are different, though think of the complexities of social behaviour among bees or ants! Even inanimate objects have relations, though they are far fewer than for a living body. You might like to think about your own relations, but be warned: it won't be a short list!

This way of thinking about the body has the immediate benefit of overcoming the dualism of biological/social that can be a problem for understanding embodiment. In this approach, all of a body's relations are important and relevant: be they physical, psychological, social or philosophical: the approach does not favour one category over another. Instead of focusing upon the body itself, in an attempt to understand what it *is*, we can consider the relations it has with the physical, social, cultural, political and ideological context, and try to describe what it *does*. This brings us back to the title of this chapter: what can a body do?

An emphasis upon a body's myriad relations is the basis for a perspective on embodiment that derives from the work of the French philosopher Gilles Deleuze and his collaborator Felix Guattari (a psychiatrist). This work has attracted much critical attention over the past twenty years as interest in the body has increased, and has been used to address many questions about embodiment (Duff 2010; Fox 2002a; 2006; Potts 2004). The rest of this chapter will be devoted to developing this perspective on the body, which will then be used in the second half of the book to make sense of embodiment, particularly in health and social care.

## What (else) a body can do

A focus on a body's relations is a focus on what a body can do (Buchanan 1997: 79). This emphasis, which emerged from Deleuze's early philosophical work on the body and identity, was applied to the area of health care in his collaborative study of mental health with Guattari (Deleuze and Guattari 1984). In their study, they asked 'what can a body do?' about those with mental health issues such as obsessive-compulsive disorders, paranoid schizophrenia and neuroses, whose behaviour can seem bizarre and often incomprehensible.

It is important to note that the question of what a body can do is not really about function, in the sense of biological structures and functions that we encountered in chapter 1. Deleuze and Guattari's method consists not in assessing bodily cause and effect (it has kidneys, so it can excrete), but in documenting the physical, psychological, emotional and other relations and attachments of a body – which may be many or few. Rather, the question should be understood as asking 'what is a body *capable* of doing?', or 'what *else* can a body do?' Another helpful question to ask is 'what are the *limits* to what a body can do?'

Deleuze and Guattari's (1984) first major collaboration looked at mental health. They suggested that people with mental health difficulties have specific limits on what their bodies can do. These are not usually physical limits; rather, the physical behaviour or interactions that occur in schizophrenia, drug use or obsessive disorders are manifestations of psychological, emotional or social limits, which are in turn a consequence of the relations that the body has acquired over time. For Deleuze and Guattari, the way to address such mental health problems is by enabling sufferers to break free from limiting relations, be these of physical, psychic or inter-personal origin. They argued that by channelling the positive, creative potential that all living beings possess, they might 'become' something more than their present limited condition.

The anti-psychiatry movement of that time may have led

Deleuze and Guattari to over-emphasize the psychological relations in mental health, and downplayed the physical causes of
mental illnesses. Yet their approach can easily encompass the
biological bases of mental health identified in recent biomedical
research. In fact it opens the way to recognizing a multi-factorial
basis: the biochemical relations of a body that may predispose
an individual to a mental health difficulty can be added to the
psychic and emotional relations that influence how that condition manifests. We can count up all these relations, regardless
of whether they are physical, psychological or cultural: the
method does not favour or deny any type of relation.

A second collaborative book broadened Deleuze and
Guattari's focus from mental health, to offer a more generalized
perspective on human embodiment as active and motivated,
rather than passive and determined (Deleuze and Guattari
1988: 149–51). They argued that what a body can *become* is of
more significance than what it 'is'. Deleuze and Guattari's aim
was not only to offer a model of embodiment, but also to show
how this could be used for physical, personal and cultural
emancipation from what they saw as the limits imposed on
the body, particularly by biomedicine and related approaches.
Their model offers the basis for an integrated understanding
of every aspect of embodiment and, in the second part of the
book, I will use this approach to explore specific aspects of the
body, including growth and ageing, health and illness, desire
and sexuality, work and care.

To fully grasp the approach to embodiment that Deleuze
and Guattari are suggesting, I will quickly look at some key
elements of their model. I will then show how this approach
can be used to explore health and identity, looking once again
at some case studies of health, illness and health care.

## The body-without-organs

For Deleuze and Guattari, the body does what it does because
of the dynamic interaction between two elements. On one hand

there are the physical and social relations that affect a body and are affected by it (Deleuze and Guattari 1994: 164). On the other, Deleuze and Guattari are keen to emphasize a body that is active, experimenting, engaged and engaging, always with the capacity to form new relations and the desire to do so (Buchanan 1997: 83). This contrasts with some of the social science descriptions in the last chapter, which can give the impression that the body is totally 'written' by human culture and the social world: that there is little room for any originality beyond the norms, values and rules of a society. In Deleuze and Guattari's model, the body is creative and engaged both biologically and socially, not a passive vehicle for the environment or the social context to mould. A body can do this and it can do that, in relation to the situations and settings it inhabits and to its aspirations within an unfolding, active experimentation. If you doubt this active principle, just observe an infant of three months or older: constantly engaging with its environment, reaching out, watchful, struggling to move around, endlessly curious, always testing the world and its own limits.

The creative force motivating the body is a feature of all living organisms, according to Deleuze and Guattari (1988: 315). A microbe, an insect, a bird or a domestic cat are all motivated in ways appropriate to their nature: to find food and an environment niche, to find a mate and reproduce, perhaps to care for their offspring. This motivation interacts with the relations to establish the limits of what the insect's or the cat's body can do. Non-human animals are guided by 'hard-wired' instincts or drives for food, shelter and reproduction, although they will also establish many other relations with other things or organisms, appropriate to their species.

For human beings, things are more complicated. As far as we know, humans are the only bodies whose brains are sufficiently complex (in terms of potential connections) to make them capable of self-consciousness and the use of abstract concepts to think and reflect upon experiences and sensations. This has enabled human bodies to affect their environment through the creation of cultural products (tools and technologies, symbolic representations of themselves and the environment, artistic creativity, and social organizations and institutions). These in turn form a myriad of relations that affect other bodies, creating and sustaining societies and cultures, complex social organization, economics, religion and politics. Generally speaking, *the more relations a body has, the more it is capable of doing.*

Deleuze and Guattari described the body that emerges from this confluence of relations and creative potential as the 'body-without-organs' (Deleuze and Guattari 1988: 149ff.), often shortened to BwO. For them, the important body is not the physical biological entity that we often think of as the 'body', especially if we are trained in biomedicine (they call this 'the organism' or the body-with-organs). From the moment of birth – perhaps even before – the BwO is constituted out of this confluence. The BwO of the newborn infant is defined largely by the drives for food, comfort and warmth, and the relations it acquires to meet these needs (with its mother, with milk, with blankets and so forth). Maturation and experience bring a multiplication of the range of relations, until for an adult human, they are myriad: physical, psychological, emotional and cultural. The discipline of the nursery and the schoolroom, the gendering and sexualization of adolescence, the routines of work and the growth and disillusionment of ageing progressively create the relations that shape the BwO and its limits. Indeed, it is useful to see the changing BwO as the limit of what a body can do at each of these stages of growth and maturation.

## Assemblages

As I noted a moment ago, in Deleuze and Guattari's model, the body is not simply 'written' by the environment and the social world, and this is an important point. Humans do not respond like computers to stimuli, but in complex and sometimes unpredictable ways that suggest an active, motivated engagement with living; the capacity to make choices and act on the world around us. Deleuze and Guattari reject the view that a body's relations (all the physical, psychological and social relations described earlier) directly determine what it can do. Rather, the relations contribute to what Deleuze and Guattari (1988: 88) call *assemblages* (*agencement* in French, meaning *arrangement*). Assemblages are the outcomes of the interaction between all of a body's relations. They develop in unpredictable ways: 'in a kind of chaotic network of habitual and non-habitual connections, always in flux, always reassembling in different ways' (Potts 2004: 19).

Assemblages are always about process: 'doing' not 'being'. Deleuze and Guattari use the metaphor of a machine to describe how assemblages connect together elements of the body with its relations (Bogue 1989: 91): they argue that every aspect of living, and our experience of the world, is comprised of these assemblages. For instance, there is an 'eating assemblage', comprising (in no particular order), at least:

mouth – food – energy – tastes or preferences;

there is a working assemblage comprising, at least:

body – task – money – career;

a sexuality assemblage comprising, at least:

sex organ – physical arousal – object of desire,

and so forth. The relations can be drawn from any of the domains, material or non-material, but in each case, you will note, the assemblage is dynamic rather than static: it is about the embodied process of eating or working or sexual desiring, not about a state of being. Furthermore, the assemblage will vary from person to person, contingent on the precise relations that exist as a consequence of experience, beliefs and attitudes, or from bodily predispositions.

The processing capacities of the human brain add

immensely to the complexity of possible assemblages. From birth, humans are immersed in a world full of cultural relations: everything from clothes (girls in pink, boys in blue!), food recipes and technologies (tools and techniques to get things done), through to customs and norms of behaviour, cultural knowledge and systems of education. These are all transmitted by material objects in the environment, but also by abstract concepts, mediated by language. The brain is progressively shaped by these complex inputs, and consequently it is impossible for human assemblages to consist merely of biological components. While a newborn infant's eating assemblage may comprise:

hunger – mouth – food

it is quickly elaborated into

hunger – mouth – food – nipple – mother

As a child's brain matures and the immersion in human culture provides the structures that enable language (and consequently the capacity for thought using abstract concepts and self-consciousness), the body gains new cultural and social relations. The eating assemblage is further elaborated into

hunger – mouth – food – tastes – mother – nipple

with the relations to nipple and mother gradually fading in importance once weaned. For the adult, however, an eating assemblage might comprise:

hunger – mouth – food – tastes – money – shopping – dietary choices – time

and many other relations particular to the context and experiences of the individual. A vegetarian's eating assemblage might include a commitment to ethics or ecology preventing meat being acceptable as a foodstuff (Fox and Ward 2008c), while that of a food allergy sufferer will involve not only a negative relation to nuts, dairy products or whatever, but also the experience of an allergic reaction. Both have emerged from an infantile relation to food, but in very different directions. These differences explain why the embodiment of one person differs from another.

We can use this model to explore processes associated with health and illness. A general health care assemblage might comprise

patient – disease – doctor – biomedicine – health technology.

There is an assemblage with particular significance for the patient with anorexia or the dieter comprising:

mouth – food – body shape – control. (Fox et al. 2005b)

Potts (2004: 22) describes an erectile dysfunction assemblage comprising:

Viagra or other pharmaceuticals – erectile dysfunction – medicalization – partners – doctors – Viagra-fied penis.

People's responses to health care are explained by the idiosyncrasies of their own particular health care assemblage. Think about Alice Martin. There is an arthritis assemblage that shapes her BwO. It comprises at least:

joints – inflammation – daily routines – pain – biomedicine – surgery – medications

But it is vastly elaborated beyond this, because of the relations Alice has with her own daily life, her memories, her desires and expectations for the future, fear of incapacity and death, as well as her circle of friends, family, carers and doctors. These relations, and how they affect Alice, create the arthritis assemblage that shapes her BwO and what (else) her body can do (the limits of her embodiment).

It is the totality of assemblages that creates the BwO and thereby the conditions of possibility for the body. Assemblages link the individual's body to the social and natural environments (Bogue 1989: 91), defining a person's capacities and her/his limits. As a consequence, bodies should be understood as neither fixed nor given, but as particular historical configurations of the material and immaterial, captured and articulated through various assemblages which to some extent determine them as particular bodies, but never manage entirely to exclude the movement of differing and the possibility of becoming otherwise. (Currier 2003: 332)

Effectively, the body is lived through the assemblages, which, as noted, are always processual: they are about doing, not being. But assemblages also *extend* the BwO far beyond the physical limits of the body: the BwO comprises non-organic as well as organic matter. Through the assemblages, our bodies-without-organs create networks between organisms, things, institutions and abstract ideas.

## Territories of the body

Every relation has the capacity to affect (or be affected by) a body, though this varies from a negligible effect to a massive one. A body might have a physical relation to gravity, a psychological relation to its parent, and a cultural relation to a nationality. In each case, associated with the relation there is a force (strong or weak) that *affects* the body. The strength of a relation's ability to affect or be affected will determine what part it plays in the assemblage. There is a gravity assemblage that affects the Earth, within which the Sun plays by far the major part, though the Moon and other planets will also affect the eventual force upon the Earth as it moves through space. For a human body, however, the gravity assemblage might also include a powerful relation to a family member, enabling a remarkable 'gravity-defying' leap to save that loved-one from danger.

Each relation thus affects (or is affected by) a body to a greater or lesser extent, and the combination of these 'affects' together determines the overall significance of each relation within the assemblages, and consequently how they shape the BwO. It follows that the BwO is a *territory* that is never static, but is sculpted by the capacity to affect and be affected by its assembled relations. There is no need to differentiate the realm from which a relation derives: physical, psychological and social relations may all play a part, with greater or lesser capacities to each affect the body. An eating assemblage might include physical resources (scarcity or plenty of specific foods), psychological preferences and tastes, and cultural restrictions such as kosher requirements. The vegetarian eating assemblage I described earlier will include physical, psychological, social and philosophical and ethical relations, with their associated forces. The outcome vector of these disparate forces limits the body to a vegetarian diet, except perhaps in circumstances where hunger becomes more dominant than ethical attachments, in which case the body will change its relation to meat and, at the same time, either relinquish ethical principles, or suffer guilt or anxiety from having transgressed those principles. The territory that the BwO inhabits depends upon the body's relations and how it affects and is affected by them.

So the BwO is the target of what Deleuze and Guattari call *territorialization* (Deleuze and Guattari 1988: 88–9) by the assemblages. The consequence may be a change in character or a re-definition. The force of the gravity assemblage territorializes the Earth as it travels through space, turning it into a 'satellite'. A biomedicine assemblage territorializes an individual consulting a health professional, transforming her/him into a patient and her/his symptoms into a disease. It follows that many aspects of human interaction involved territorialization, with one or both parties affected. Territories and territorializations are often concerned with socially created meanings: philosophy and ideology have historically territorialized land as 'nations', Homeland or Fatherland (Deleuze and Guattari 1994: 68).

However, all forces can be resisted, partly or totally. The Earth does not succumb entirely to the Sun's gravitational pull, because its velocity through space acts as a counter-force that always seeks to escape and move away on its own trajectory.

The resultant orbit is the vector of force and counter-force. Because forces add and subtract from each other, it is possible for one force to *de-territorialize* a territorialized BwO. It is also possible for another force to then *re-territorialize* the BwO again. The BwO is thus both the site where the body's relations territorialize it, but also the site of resistance and refusal. In this way, the BwO is constructed and reconstructed (territorialized) continually, as forces interact within the assemblages. For example, an individual consulting a health professional may resist and refuse the patient role and find an alternative embodiment, such as a 'consumer' of health services (Fox and Ward 2006). In Alice Martin's case, despite the territorialization of her body by arthritis, she also draws on resources (relations) of strength from friends, family and her own desire for independence, to resist the disease and find ways to remain active, including working for an arthritis charity. She may have a home help who can aid her in this, providing not only physical assistance with cooking or dressing, but also with psychological support or 'just' friendship. I will have much more to say about the capacity of carers to 'de-territorialize' their clients in this way in chapter 7.

As a model of embodiment, territorialization provides an explanatory framework for how social relations impinge on individuals or cultures, from class, gender and ethnic stratification (see chapter 6) through to the creation of subjectivities in people as, for instance, 'women', 'husbands', 'patients' and 'risk takers'. However, Deleuze and Guattari always recognize the capacity of the body to resist these forces, re-shaping how relations interact within the assemblages that constitute the BwO.

Humans have devised tools and technologies to counter many physical territorializations of the body (a Scuba suit will allow a human body to breathe under water, a bike will allow us to travel faster than on foot); psychological and cultural territorialization (for instance, a gender role or a professional duty) may actually be harder to resist. Here, human beings' capacity to re-interpret the world with infinite variety is of importance: systems of thought in politics, religion and social science reflect the potential we have to reject and resist one territorialization (for instance, male dominance in the workplace), and impose another re-territorialization (for example, feminism). Resistance, be it the refusal by a child to acquiesce to its parents' wishes, or the rejection by a progressive social movement (for example, the anti-apartheid movement in South Africa) of ideas, power and control by a dominant group, reflects this capacity of the body to re-shape its assemblages and 'become-other'.

## The body *with* organs and beyond

One territorialization that is of particular relevance for those engaged in health care is the biomedical body that we explored in chapter 1. The body-*with*-organs is the name that Deleuze and Guattari give to this commonplace biological body, which they also call the 'organism' (Deleuze and Guattari 1988: 158). The body-*with*-organs is the product of powerful forces emanating from biomedicine, inherent in the medicalizing processes of health care that turn bodies into patients, and their experiences of their sick bodies into case histories of disease. The sick, the convalescent, the disabled are all part of this territorialization: the history of health has been written and continues to be written within the biomedical territory. Criticism of the body-*with*-organs lies at the heart of Deleuze and Guattari's (1984) writing on mental illness, but there is also a long and strong and broad tradition of anti-medicalization in social science writing on health and illness (for example, Abraham 2010; Clarke et al. 2003; Conrad 2007).

However, the model of the body that I have developed in this chapter suggests that the body-*with*-organs is just one territorialization of the body among many. Social science models of the body (including what you are reading at this moment) are rival territorializations: each of the approaches described in chapter 2 seeks to show how social and cultural forces construct our bodies. The concept of territorialization is useful as a reminder of the multitude of forces in the natural and social worlds that impinge on bodies, but also, importantly, of the possibility of resisting these forces. While it is unquestionable that bodies are the subjects of physical and biological forces, the point about the body-*with*-organs or 'the organism' is that it has become a very powerful model of the body, to the extent that it can be hard to imagine an alternative, particularly when the subject of this territorialization is sick, vulnerable and dependent on health professionals who use this model of the body to inform their work and their interactions with patients.

We can understand the 'patient' and her/his health/illness as a territorialization (by relations, forces and assemblages) of a *body-without-organs* into a body-*with*-organs, a body defined by biomedicine and limited by this definition as to what it can do. What a patient's body can do is not a matter of health assessment or pathology diagnosis, an exercise in assessing mobility or capacity to work or to reason or whatever, but of exploring the limits of what *else* it can do, in the sense of how it is psychologically, socially and culturally, as well as physically, territorialized. Thus, for instance, Alice Martin's arthritis has had a secondary impact upon her: because it has been defined in medical terms and has drawn Alice into the realm of doctors, hospital, medicines and surgery, it has opened her BwO to a powerful biomedicine assemblage that has transformed her into a patient, and her pain and lack of mobility into a disease to be analysed, diagnosed and treated medically. Resisting such a biomedical assemblage is remarkably difficult in a culture in which biomedicine is so dominant.

Part of Deleuze and Guattari's project was to undermine dominant territorializations, including the body-*with*-organs. They wanted to show how it is possible to resist territorialization and to find what they called a *line of flight* from that territorialization to a new state of embodiment. This can happen by introducing a new force, or strengthening an already present weak force. In relation to mental health, Deleuze and Guattari (1984) called this process 'schizoanalysis'; more generally as a strategy for living, they called it 'nomadology' (Deleuze and Guattari 1988). Inevitably, any new state of embodiment after a line of flight is also a re-territorialization, but it may be one where a body can do more (or different things) than it could do in its previous territorialization. Challenging a biomedical territorialization of the body as the body-*with*-organs might help patients to pursue an aspiration, or open locked doors to new vistas (Buchanan 1997: 85). Importantly, this

> does not result in the patient being restored to his or her former self, rather, using the newly awakened affect, he or she is encouraged to invent a new self. (Buchanan 1997: 85)

This is important for health care professionals, as they, and the care they provide, can be the relation that may either de-territorialize a person or patient, helping them to move beyond the current limits of their embodiment, or re-territorialize them, typically by defining them narrowly in biomedical terms (Fox 1993: 84ff.). Care can be an invaluable resource to enable a line of flight from the physical and psychological limits of a chronic illness or disability, as we will see in chapter 7.

## The body and identity

Sociologists of the body have recognized that embodiment contributes to establishing a sense-of-self, 'subjectivity' or 'identity' (Darke 1996; Featherstone and Hepworth 1991; Fox and Ward 2008b). The 'doing' body, lived from moment to moment, provides a basis for who we are, and also opportunities to display our identity; be this in terms of gender or sexuality, our employment or social class, our allegiances to a social group and so forth. In Bourdieu's (1984) terms, the body can be a means to make itself 'distinct' from others.

Few theorists would now claim that human identity is inherent (for a full discussion of theories of identity, see Jenkins

1996). Rather, it seems that the sense we have of ourselves (and our capacity to reflect on who we are and what we wish to become) emerges gradually during childhood and into adult life as a consequence of interactions with our social and cultural environment (Massumi 1992: 68ff.) and the development of language. This is not a once-and-for-all event: Goffman (1968, 1990) suggested that the identity could be 'stripped away' in surroundings such as hospitals or asylums where routines and bureaucracy reduced a person's autonomy and independence. In the context of the experience of chronic illness, Charmaz argues that

> Physical pain, psychological distress, and the deleteri-ous effects of medical procedures all cause the chronically ill to suffer as they experience their illness. However, a narrow medicalized view of suffering ignores or minimizes the broader significance of suffering: the *loss of self* felt by many people with chronic illnesses. Chronically ill people frequently experience a crumbling away of their former self-images without simultaneous development of equally valued new ones. (Charmaz 1983: 168, emphasis in original)

From a different perspective, Foucault (1976, 1979) saw insti-tutions such as the hospital, the prison, education and the workplace as actually creating subjectivities in those who are the object of their regimes (see chapter 6). For him, there was no possibility of an identity that was free from the world that surrounds an individual: the discipline that the school, prison or hospital imposes on the body of a person creates an identity as 'scholar', 'prisoner', or 'patient'. The theoretical framework developed by Deleuze and Guattari and set out in this chap-ter has something in common with Foucault's understanding of the body and the self, but sees more scope to resist these imposed identities through de-territorialization and lines of flight.

The Deleuzian view of the relationship between body and identity suggests that as a person develops more and more relations and (aided by language acquisition and consequent admission into human culture) progressively more complex assemblages during childhood and into adult life, selfhood stabilizes from a myriad of possible identities (Ansell Pearson 1999; Buchanan 1997; Currier 2003; Fox 2002a; Massumi 1992; Potts 2004). Gender identity, for example, depends not only upon possessing male or female sex organs, but also role models and stereotypes, as well as early experiences, as we will see in chapter 5. Identification with parents and subsequent rebellion are part of self-development throughout childhood, as assemblages incorporate more and more elements.

For Deleuze, identity is never fixed, nor is it some kind of pure 'essence' of who we are, but an outcome of bodies in relationship. The experience of self, of 'I' comes into being through an assemblage of relations, and

> . . . consists of a changeable collection of fragments among which the struggle between powers and resistances takes place. A panorama of possible experiences, modes of conduct and reactions opens up. The 'I' is not a unity but a wide range of experiences, intentions, desires, powers, movements, souls and the like. (Huijer 1999: 65–6)

Understanding identity or 'sense-of-self' as the confluence ('running-together') of an assemblage with the creative energies of the body means that self is intimately linked to embodiment and the relations a body has. For humans, identity emerges in the context of the body's relations, from the moment of birth onwards, out of countless possible selves (Massumi 1992: 76). Some relations in early life may be key to how we see ourselves, though throughout life our identities may modify and develop as other body relations and capacities to affect and be affected become part of the identity assemblage. Identities may be productive or destructive, but are always amenable to modification.

Critical to the establishment of an identity are those moments of self-reflection in which something (a deterritorialization) triggers a moment of awareness: 'So it's me!' So that's what it's about!' (Deleuze and Guattari 1984: 19–20; Bogue 1989: 95). Most of the time, this does not radically disrupt the assemblages patterning the BwO: they soon settle back into comfortable and familiar paths (Deleuze and Guattari 1988: 56). Occasionally, we may experience a more dramatic de-territorialization that can push off in a new direction. The diagnosis of a chronic illness such as osteoarthritis, Parkinson's disease or multiple sclerosis could be just such a moment, radically transforming an independent identity into dependency (Pinder 1992).

Identity is thus an active, creative process, driven by 'the capacity to form new relations, and the desire to do so' (Buchanan 1997: 83), and thus intimately associated with embodiment (Fox and Ward 2006). For Deleuze and Guattari, the character of subjectivity derives from what the body does (and what *else* it can do – what it can *become*). In the second part of this book, I will explore how body and self interact in relation to different aspects of embodiment. Thus in chapter 4, I will look at health and illness and the different embodied identities that are possible in relation to medical and non-medical perspectives on health. Chapter 5 looks at different aspects of desire, from consumption to sexuality, while the next considers how the body is managed in the workplace, school and hospital. Chapter 6 also looks in greater detail at bodies and 'health identities': the assemblages that establish sense-of-self in relation to health, development and ageing. I consider health care from the perspective of both carers and the cared-for in chapter 7 and look at the interactions between bodies, technology and identity in the final chapter. In all of these areas, I will look at the close association between body and self, and the effects of identity on how we experience our bodies.

## Beyond bodies with organs

In this chapter I have introduced a key approach to the body that moves beyond the false dualism of biology and the social sciences. In this conclusion, I will pick out the key elements of the model and once again consider some case studies of embodiment.

The first important aspect to Deleuze and Guattari's model or embodiment concerns what a body is. A clear distinction has been drawn in this chapter between the common-sense body of biology and a wider sense of embodiment that incorporates the natural and social worlds, and the biology and the social aspects of a body. The use of the term *body-without-organs* (BwO) makes this clearer. The BwO is the limit of what a body can do, not in a functionalist sense, but in terms of its relations and the play of forces of those relations. For patients, people with disabilities, older adults and for anyone, the social and the natural worlds may territorialize the BwO, to establish limits from which it is hard to escape. But these limits can be re-drawn, especially if one has a little help. The BwO emerges from the multiplicity of physical, psychological and social relations of a body, and the play of these forces within body assemblages.

We looked at Alice Martin and the relations that she has with her environment. They are of course myriad, and include the physical relations of a biological entity to oxygen, nutrition, warmth and light, and so forth. Alice's long life has provided many experiences, which have contributed to her memories and to her psychological attachments: to family and friends, to preferences and tastes, and to attitudes and beliefs. There are cultural relations to her sense of her nationality, her gender and her class and ethnicity, and philosophical relations to ideas and values. As she has grown older, her body's physical relations have been affected by a general 'slowing-down'; osteo-arthritis has changed her abilities to undertake some tasks, and also had a psychological effect on her sense of independence. It has also limited her ability to engage fully in the social networks around her. Ageing can also affect how we see ourselves, and perhaps Alice still feels like a 20-year-old, but the woman she sees in the mirror may be at odds with this feeling.

The second element of the model emphasizes that embodiment is not the passive outcome of 'inscription' by these relations and forces, but a dynamic, reflexive 'reading' of the social by an active, experimenting, motivated life-force. For Deleuze and Guattari, the BwO is like an uncharted territory, but one whose possession must be fought over, inch by inch. It is always in flux, as it is endlessly territorialized, de-territorialized and re-territorialized. Assemblages lead to territorialization, but because of this active, motivated, and 'experimenting' life-force, territorializations can be resisted and subverted. This dynamic model of embodiment can conjure the endless permutations of living: of health, illness, sexual desire, ageing and death, the multiplying, becoming-other body that is always capable of a new interpretation, another nuance.

So Alice is not simply the victim of the changing relations of embodiment that come with disability and ageing. She may experience difficulty in some tasks that she could do easily when more fit, but that does not mean she has abandoned her struggle against these obstacles. Alice chooses not to acquiesce, but to find ways to continue to resist the effects of arthritis. Working as a volunteer for an arthritis charity is one way she has continued to de-territorialize her BwO, enabling her to look beyond her immediate circumstances. She uses her resources to avoid territorialization into disability. Interactions with the health professions are as an equal, not as a dependant.

Finally, the body is intimately linked with identity in Deleuze and Guattari's model. Identity is a feature of the clustering of relations around specific aspects of embodiment, such as health, gender, sport and exercise, body modification, disability or growing old. Just as embodiment emerges from activity and practice (what a body can do), so does a sense of self. Both are located within the totality of a body's physical and social relations. For Alice, her sense of herself is in flux, and perhaps in some ways she is no longer the person she was before her arthritis developed. The relations with her physical body and with the health professions she encounters, and the changing relations with her family and friends, or with the charity she supports, together determine her present sense of who she is, and what her life is about. Her identity is fully embodied, an outcome of the assemblages that establish the limits of what (else) her body can do. Her identity has not 'crumbled away' because of her illness, but has changed to accommodate the new relations of her BwO.

These three elements of the model of embodiment set out here will be used in the second part of the book to explore the body and associated identities, beginning with health and illness.

### Suggested further reading

Buchanan, I. (1997) The problem of the body in Deleuze and Guattari, or, what can a body do? *Body and Society*, 3, 73–91.

Duff, C. (2010) Towards a developmental ethology: exploring Deleuze's contribution to the study of health and human development. *Health*, 14 (6), 619–34.

Fox, N. J. (1999) *Beyond Health. Postmodernism and Embodiment.* London: Free Association Books.

# CHAPTER FOUR

# The Body in Health and Illness

The natural and the cultural aspects of embodiment are inextricably linked within health and illness. We can often identify an underlying pathology causing disease, degeneration or other impairment in a body, but the experience of being ill and the social responses to health and illness require understanding of the contexts in which bodies act. Think for a moment about what health means to you: how do you define this idea that is so often taken for granted?

If you struggle to offer a useful definition you are not alone. Biomedicine sees health as merely an absence of disease, and this view is often the dominant one. The World Health Organization (WHO 1985) offers a more holistic, if rather vague definition, considering health to be a state of 'complete physical, mental and social well-being'. From an anthropological perspective, Wright (1982) sees health as 'what it is to function as a human', with illness occurring when the body fails to function but continues to be seen as human. Canguilhem (1989) defines health and illness as positive and negative biological values. Illness is marked by increasing dependency, suggests de Swaan (1990: 220), while health represents a 'maximization of potential and expression in everyday activities of life' according to Anderson (1991: 109).

Health and illness have psychological and emotional components. For instance, pain and its control may be a key determinant of the experience of being ill, as may knowledge of the severity of a condition, or a family history of the illness. Our social and cultural context may also have implications for whether a body is considered healthy or sick. What do you think our social norms concerning mobility or sexual activity at different ages might say about whether individuals aged 10, 25 or 80 are considered 'healthy' or not? Different cultures may respond differently to episodes of an illness, perhaps cosseting the sick, or alternatively expecting them to 'pull themselves together'. This means that we cannot accept health and illness simply as features of the biological body, nor accept unthinkingly the phenomena of birth, growth, death and disease as 'natural'.

Although the words *disease* and *illness* are sometimes used interchangeably in everyday talk, we can use them more precisely. So we can distinguish between *disease* as a biological state resulting from an infection, an organic, genetic or systemic defect or some other divergence from a biomedically defined norm of bodily function, and *illness* as our personal bodily and psychological experience of suffering from this disease or defect (Eisenberg 1977: 11). The anthropologist Arthur Kleinman (1978) uses a third term: *sickness*, to describe the social response to an episode of illness (for instance, whether it is considered legitimate grounds for release from normal work or domestic duties, or what kind of care a society provides to sufferers). Societies may define health in various ways, and politics and economics can play a part too (for instance, where illness may entitle a person to a status or a financial benefit). I will use this three-way definition of disease/illness/sickness to unpack health and the body.

In the context of a book about embodiment, this chapter considers health and illness not as states of being, but as embodied processes defining what (else) a body can do. Using the model of embodiment developed in the first part of the book, I will look first at the biomedical approach to disease and the emergence of the hospital clinic as a focus on bodies in health and disease. I then consider the material, psychological and social relations that a body can have concerning disease, illness and sickness, and how these constitute assemblages that define the body-without-organs (BwO) in health and illness. I will also look at the ageing process, to understand the important relation that a body has with time, and how this is accepted or resisted. Along the way, I consider the messages for health care professionals as they work with people in health and illness, applying the case study of Alice Martin.

## Health and the body-*with*-organs

Although I argued in the last chapter that it is more important to ask what a body *does* than what it *is,* bodies are continually subjected to forces in its environment that try to define it and determine its character. Bodies are in the front line when it comes to people's judgements about those they meet. Bodies are defined and disciplined as male or female, black or white, attractive or unattractive, healthy or sick, young or old. Many consumer products are also aimed directly at bodies. Just imagine walking down your local high street or shopping mall and you can quickly visualize the multitude of body specialists offering body goods and services: clothing, shoes and fashion; hairdressers; pharmacists, cosmetic dentists and opticians; beauty and cosmetics goods and services. These all offer to mould our bodies into one form or another. Meanwhile, the popular media sustain an obsession with body shape and size, particularly where bodies belong to 'celebrities' or those in the public eye. Social and cultural forces within institutions such as schools and hospitals, and cultural movements such as youth cultures or political groups, may also encourage efforts to make a body one thing or another.

The body is a focus for the work or the concerns of various professions, and consequently of the academic and scientific descriptions of the body and embodiment that have developed to inform these professional groups. Theology and religion were probably the earliest examples of a professional interest in the body. The Jewish scriptures known as the *Torah* (which also supply the Christian Old Testament) had much to say about what bodies can and cannot do: from sexual practices to guidelines on daily worship to dietary prohibitions; and laws and guidance on bodily behaviour are features of most world religions today. Secular law-makers adapted some of these religious rules to create legal codes that define what a body may or may not do legitimately, and what counts as a 'crime'. In every society, killing another human body is a criminal act, although provocation, self-defence or wartime action may all be partial or total justifications. Bodies have also been the focus for the punishment of offenders, from imprisonment, mutilation and torture, to execution and transportation.

Early physicians such as Hippocrates and Galen were not far behind the priests and lawyers in their development of a body perspective. They founded a medical 'discourse' on the body that has been elaborated to the present day, so that many features of embodiment are now the subject of a medical interest, from the normal and abnormal functioning of organs and cells, through to advice on health behaviour and risk avoidance. Foucault (1976) described the development of this discourse in the past three hundred years, as modern hospitals emerged as the location for observation of the body, and the establishment of an archive in which the biomedical body is fully documented. Primary care and public health have extended this approach into the community (Armstrong 1983). This discourse has also entered the popular domain, and medical advice or self-help books about the biomedical body are legion. These ideas about the body and health create the biomedicalized 'body-*with*-organs' (Deleuze and Guattari 1988: 158), in which biology and the medical sciences define the body in health and illness. I will have more to say about Foucault's analysis of the body and discipline in chapter 6.

I want, however, to explore the body in health and illness from a different perspective, taking as a starting point not the body-*with*-organs, but the body-*without*-organs, and the question first set out in the last chapter: what (else) can a healthy or a sick body do? I will start this analysis by looking at a body's relations and the assemblages these construct.

Taking the three-way distinction between disease, illness and sickness, I will look at how the body is affected by different realms of relations, before drawing these together to explore the assemblages that constitute the body in health and illness.

## Body relations, health and illness

In the first part of the book, I showed how there is more to a body than its biology and that the body is inevitably both biological and social. These different realms of relations contribute to the shaping of those aspects of embodiment (assemblages) that we call health and illness. It is the interplay of these realms that constitute what a body can do, or to put it another way, the limits of the body-without-organs. So let us now look at the relations and assemblages of relations that pattern a body and its 'disease', its 'illness' and its 'sickness', before asking the harder question of what constitutes a body's 'health'.

### The body and disease

Disease, you will recall, is a medically defined category. For modern medicine, diseases 'are abnormalities in the function and/or structure of body organs and systems' (Eisenberg 1977: 9). Diseases may be caused by an external agency such as an infection, or an environmental influence such as a toxin, pollution or poor diet, or even a psychological stressor such as damp or over-crowded housing or social disorder. Alternatively disease may be a consequence of some systemic failure which may have a physiological, biochemical or genetic origin, or can be the result of trauma or other injury to cells or organs. Finally, diseases may be the outcome of progressive deterioration or degeneration, as can be seen in ageing, or in diseases such as multiple sclerosis and Parkinson's disease.

These descriptions are all part of the modern biomedical model that we have already explored at some length in chapter 1. Other healing systems (for instance, Chinese medicine or homoeopathy) also use models of disease, although the elements may be quite different. Acupuncture, for instance, describes a network of body meridians that influence disease and its treatment. These rival systems of disease have in common that they seek to describe the objective factors that determine the cause, natural history, prognosis and treatment of an episode of disease. Kleinman (1980) called these systems 'explanatory models'. They also have in common that they are systems used by professional healers (both Western biomedical professionals and other traditional healers) to define and justify their judgements about causation, prognosis and treatment.

So we can identify the various relations that a body has which together contribute to its 'disease'. In terms of the physical and biological relations, the most obvious is an infective agency: a virus or a bacterium. Relations with gravity (leading to falls or other accidents) and with any number of objects that might cause trauma can also be relevant material relations. The environment plays a role in degenerative disease. In our case study, the passage of time and the effect of relentless wear on Alice Martin's joints have contributed to her arthritic disease. Ageing is in part the action of time on a physical entity that will eventually deteriorate and die. Other environment factors in the workplace or the home can also result in accidents or progressive disease such as silicosis, or can influence psychological or emotional disease. Within the biomedical disease model, none of these factors in themselves determine disease: exposure to a bacterium does not guarantee infection, but coupled with lowered bodily resistance or immunity and perhaps a genetic predisposition, it may lead to a disease state. These factors together contribute to the assemblage that will determine the outcome and pattern of subsequent health or disease.

We can also identify psychological relations with things or people that impact on disease. There is evidence that a person's relationships can have profound effects on both physical and psychological well-being. Immunity can be compromised by psychological stress resulting in vulnerability to infection. Brown and Harris (1978) found that stressors in the environment can lead to mental health problems such as depression, as can the challenges of caring for young children, or loss of a parent during childhood. However, support from a close friend or family can protect against the stresses of daily life. It has been claimed that a positive mental attitude (that is, positive relations to people or events in one's environment) can help to overcome diseases, including cancer (Dalton et al. 2002). Think about the last time you had a bout of illness such as a cold or flu: how did you feel psychologically? Did you try to keep a positive attitude to speed your recovery, or feel depressed you were missing out on your daily life?

Health behaviours grounded in psychological or emotional responses to the environment or others will affect the onset or severity of disease: diet, smoking, alcohol and drug use and unsafe sexual behaviour may all increase the risks of disease. Disease may also alter a person's psychological responses to others, either making them withdrawn or more dependent. Diseases themselves may be psychological or emotional: depression, anxiety and schizophrenia are all conditions defined in terms of a biomedical model, and may be treated through physical or psychological therapies.

There can be social relations that affect disease. It is well-established that social deprivation, most notably poverty, poor housing, unemployment and poor diet, along with socially determined norms concerning health behaviours may all increase the likelihood of disease (Davey-Smith et al. 2002; Townsend and Davidson 1990). Cultural practices may enhance or inhibit disease in particular ethnic or social groups, from the use of toxic inebriants such as *khat* among Somalis, through to prohibitions on certain treatments such as blood transfusions by Jehovah's Witnesses (a Christian sect). A lack of relations may also affect disease: social isolation has been shown to be a factor in increasing susceptibility to mental and physical ill-health (Cacioppo and Hawkley 2003; House et al.

1988). For Alice, arthritis has brought isolation due to limits on her physical mobility and fewer outings to friends or the shops.

Therapies to treat diseases may involve relations that are material, psychological or social. The main material or biological relations are with pharmacological therapeutics, physical therapies, prosthetics and other medical devices. The treatment of a disease may also simply entail managing a disordered metabolism, or by surgical intervention. For some diseases, treatment may only have the goal of stopping or slowing progression, or treating symptoms. Time also is a great healer, as the saying goes!

*The body and illness*
Illness, in the definition that we set out earlier to distinguish it from disease, is concerned with the experience of the sufferer, rather than the objective fact of disease as defined by a health professional. It is experienced through symptoms, which may be physical, psychological or social, as opposed to the signs that a health care professional may seek out (Foucault 1976: 93; Kleinman 1988: 16). Pain, unusual sensations, changes to normal mobility or energy levels, or more extreme symptoms such as bleeding, signify to the sufferer a divergence from a state of health, independent of any specialist knowledge of biology, physiology or biochemistry. Illness need not have a one-to-one relationship with disease. As Eisenberg (1977: 11) points out:

> ... disease may occur in the absence of illness: the person with hypertension may be asymptomatic and therefore unconcerned when the physician who measures his blood pressure becomes alarmed; he may stop taking the prescribed medication because it makes him 'ill', even though he is told it will mitigate his 'disease'. Only when the hypertension leads to congestive failure or hemiplegia will the person become a patient.

On occasions, illness occurs without the presence of a disease that can be identified by a professional. Sufferers may in such

circumstances be stigmatized as malingerers or hypochondri-
acs. But I am sure that from time to time you have felt 'under
the weather', with no obvious disease affecting you. US students in the 1960s might succumb to 'brain fag', a loss of
concentration caused by studying too hard!

In many cases, however, illness and disease do coincide, in
the sense that a person may experience a deviation from their
normal experience of their body, and a professional might
subsequently discern what s/he might call an underlying disease. There is a significant difference, however: a person may
experience a fever, while a professional might diagnose an
infection; a lay person may feel 'blue', but a psychiatrist might
label it as 'reactive depression'. Illness is filtered through the
subjectivity and self-awareness of the person who is experiencing it, rather than through the lens of a biomedical model. To
use Kleinman's (1980) terminology again, the lay person has
a different 'explanatory model' from the professional's. The
lay person experiences a runny nose, a cough, and a feeling
of low energy, and calls it 'the flu', while the professional gaze
over that body elicits signs of infection and diagnoses an upper
respiratory tract infection which may or not be caused by an
influenza virus.

The difference is that, for lay people (I resist calling them
'patients' here, as this is a medical category) an illness is part
of the entire context of her/his life. Alice Martin does not
think about physiology or biochemistry, but about what she
can and cannot do, for instance, whether she can go to the
shops, look after her family or live independently. From a professional point of view, by contrast, the agenda focuses on the
physical body, and on curing disease or minimizing its effects.
They may see a patient like Alice in a hospital or a GP surgery and not notice much more than the disease itself. While
lay and professional perspectives thus have some relations
in common, the lay illness assemblage and the professional
disease assemblage also contain relations that are exclusive to
themselves.

The body's illness relations are typically psychological and social. Psychologically and emotionally, the relations concern the interpretation of symptoms or diagnoses: the experiences of conditions suffered by family members or other associates may colour what an illness episode means for someone. Pinder (1992: 14) described the impact of a diagnosis of Parkinson's disease (PD) on one patient:

> Both Mr D's mother and grandmother had had PD, yet his own identity was suddenly transformed by the news. He had, all of a sudden, become a 'Shaky Bill' . . . he was experiencing what it was like at first hand.

In a study of older adults (Fox 2005), the impact of ill-health had a significant impact on the day-to-day experience of living for one respondent, Mrs C.

> You think about old times, that's when you ask 'Why should it be me?' People at my age are still going like anything and I can't, that's what gets me down. You see people of 80 getting round, good as gold, not me. I've just got to put up with what I've got. If I could get around more, I wouldn't be here, not yet. The doctor reckons it's hereditary. My dad died of a heart attack; my brother had an operation on the heart; my sister's had an operation . . . I live from day to day now.

Relations to hazards in the environment may also influence health and illness behaviour. Behaviours that seem irrational from a disease perspective can be the outcome of weighing up risks and benefits: smoking may provide the mental support to cope with the immediate pressures of life; using street drugs may provide a high that outweighs the risks of side-effects or death (Fox 2002b).

Psychological and emotion relations also play a role in the treatment and management of illness. These relations may include health care professionals: dependency or trust in a health professional can contribute to a patient's recovery from illness (de Swaan 1990; Kleinman 1988), or to a positive experience of care (Fox 1999: 90ff.). Compliance with the advice offered by a professional may depend upon this kind of positive relationship, and will also depend upon how the advice complements a person's own evaluation of the illness, its cause and its management (Butler et al. 1996; Kinmonth et al. 1998). Bissell et al. (2004) suggest that health professionals should tailor their advice to meet the expectations of their patients. Associated with this is the 'placebo' effect: during recovery from disease, belief in the efficacy of a cure may improve outcomes, regardless of any physical properties of the treatment (Macedo et al. 2003). Here relations to theories and beliefs may be powerful factors in how illness is experienced. I will consider these issues more fully when I look at caring bodies in chapter 7.

There are numerous social relations affecting illness, in addition to the epidemiological factors influencing disease patterns noted earlier. The perception, experience and coping with illness depends upon cultural explanations of disease (explanatory models), which are contingent upon age, ethnicity, gender, education and so forth (Kleinman et al. 2006: 141). For example, Zola (1966) argued that Irish Americans showed a more stoical response to pain or an episode of illness compared with those of Italian origin, because of their different backgrounds and expectations during illness. Friends, family and care professionals may be consulted and involved in an episode of ill-health, from onset of symptoms onwards. According to Kleinman et al. (2006), most illness episodes are managed without reference to formal health services, so relations with family, self-help groups, religious practitioners and other healers will all affect the experience of illness.

*The body and sickness*
In the three-way definition of disease, illness and sickness, the last term refers to how the social and cultural context affects how illness is manifested. Cultural beliefs affect how people communicate health problems, how symptoms are experi-

enced and presented, who is consulted, how long they stay in care, and how they evaluate their care (Kleinman et al. 2006: 141). The GP and anthropologist Cecil Helman described lay beliefs held by Londoners about how to treat minor infections and fevers, which were unrelated to the biology of these conditions. People felt colds were caused by cold, damp forces, which could move around the body, from nose to throat to lungs, while fevers were caused by hot, dry forces (Helman 1978). In my study of older adults (Fox 2005), culture had an immense impact on experience of ill-health: many Australians found the loss of independence hard to bear, while for Thai elders, Buddhism and a stronger family network meant that being cared for was a positive experience.

However, culture also affects the social organization and management of disease, and hence social, political and economic relations impinge upon the sick body. In Western medicine, health care is dominated by biomedicine, while in other countries and in earlier times, folk remedies and traditional healers played a more important role in managing illness. Health care services may be free at the point of delivery (as in the UK) or paid for privately or by health insurance (as in the US and much of Europe). These relations may be important in determining uptake of health care, and the character of the relationship between health professional and client. Illness thus occurs in a context in which political and economic relations may affect the sick body.

In a work-oriented culture such as the West, health is prized as a requisite for productivity, while illness is seen as limiting. Disability campaigners have argued that the social response to a physical or mental impairment is more debilitating than the underlying problem itself: Goffman (1968) described how disabled people had a 'master identity' thrust upon them that overwhelms other attributes or abilities. Similarly, conditions such as a birth mark or dependency on a wheelchair or prosthesis could be stigmatizing: leading to real or perceived prejudice. A contemporary example might be obesity, where the negative cultural response may be experienced very power-fully by overweight people (Schwartz et al. 2003). At 75, Alice Martin has retired from the world of work, and with arthritis limiting her social interactions, she is slowly disappearing out of the social world. For many older people, their contribution to society may seem less and less important as they age and become sick.

Finally, the role of health and medical professionals and responses to them by patients are governed by social and cultural norms, as are responses to therapies and health technologies. Kleinman et al. (2006: 141) argue that

> biomedicine is primarily interested in the recognition and treatment of disease (curing). So paramount is this ori-entation that the professional training of doctors tends to disregard illness and its treatment. Biomedicine has increas-ingly banished the illness experience as a legitimate object of clinical concern. Carried to its extreme, this orientation, so successful in generating technological interventions, leads to a veterinary practice of medicine.

This focus on disease at the expense of illness experience is part of the phenomenon of medicalization, in which more and more aspects of life (from pregnancy and childbirth, to sexual function, diet and body shape) are becoming the focus of a medical perspective. I will look at medicalization in more detail in chapter 8.

## The ill-health assemblage

I have described in some detail the many relations that a body may have during ill-health, affecting the body in disease, ill-ness and sickness. We have also seen the work of forces (for instance, the power of biomedicine to define disease states, or the effects of culture on how illness is experienced and managed). The intensity of each relation is important, from the virulence of an infective relation through to the power of a cultural determinant of how care is managed. The severity of disease, the impact of the experience of illness and the effect upon the body of cultural factors will determine the overall effect on the body.

All three elements are important in ill-health: the body will always have relations in each of the three domains of disease, illness and sickness simultaneously, though their impact may vary according to circumstances (for an unconscious patient, there will be no experience of illness, though disease and sickness relations will still affect the body). All three sets of relations contribute to what we might call an *ill-health assemblage*. This assemblage shapes the *becoming-sick* or *sickening body*, which is the body-without-organs (BwO) of ill-health. The ill-health assemblage determines the limits of what (else) the body can do during ill-health.

What does an ill-health body assemblage look like? The answer to this is that it is hugely variable, always unique to the individual body, and of course dependent upon the features of the disease and the wider social contexts of the experience of illness. It is therefore easier to look at specifics rather than generalities, and you might like to look back now at the outline of an arthritis body assemblage described toward the end of chapter 3.

An ill-health assemblage is constituted from the multiplicity of physical, psychological and social relations and affects that surround a body during an episode of ill-health. At its simplest, we could imagine an assemblage comprising:

virus – immune system – organ – body signs and symptoms

However, for an adult, many other psychosocial and cultural relations will contribute, for instance:

organ – disease – doctor – biomedicine – health care system –
health technology – daily responsibilities – pain – fear.

Ill-health is shaped by these relations, which can have as much to do with the emotional meaning of illness and the cultural contexts of ill-health as with the disease itself. As noted earlier, there is an assemblage with particular significance for the patient with anorexia or the dieter comprising:

mouth – food – body shape – control (Fox et al. 2005)

Potts (2004: 22) describes an impotence treatment assemblage that includes the penis, the sufferer's partner, doctors, and Viagra or other pharmaceuticals. Table 4.1 categorizes the different types of disease, illness and sickness relations that may contribute to the ill-health assemblage.

| Table 4.1. Relations comprising the ill-health assemblage | | | |
|---|---|---|---|
| | *Physical and biological* | *Psychological and emotional* | *Socio-cultural and philosophical* |
| 'Disease' | Genetic diseases Pathogens Time, ageing and degenerative diseases Pollutants and environmental hazards Impaired immunity Therapeutics, physical therapies and prostheses | Environmental stressors Health behaviours Psychological and neurological diseases | Biomedicine Health care professionals Social deprivation Cultural practices 'Life events' Social isolation Public health and epidemiology Health technology providers |
| 'Illness' | Pain Placebos | Health, illness and risk behaviour Health beliefs Psychological therapies Trust and compliance | Culturally specific explanatory models Lay networks and folk remedies Popular culture health representations |
| 'Sickness' | Pain Stigmatizing symptoms or impairments | Fear and other emotional responses to ill-health Dependency and independence | Biomedical model of health and illness Cultural expectations of health and illness Social organization and management of disease Economics and politics of health care and technology Social attitudes to health and illness |

Ill-health assemblages are not just constituted from these generalized relations. There will also be many relations and affects unique to the setting, circumstances, past experiences and other aspects of illness: people's differing responses to illness and to health care are explained by the idiosyncrasies of their own particular ill-health assemblage. Ill-health assemblages will also vary depending on how diseases and illnesses are understood, or upon the institutions that cater for the sick. Try reading Jane Austen's *Sense and Sensibility* for an insight into a Georgian ill-health assemblage, in which forces of disease can strike at times of emotional imbalance, thrusting a body into fever and possible death. Foucault's (1971) history of mental illness *Madness and Civilization* demonstrates the various assemblages surrounding mental health in past times, when madness was often feared and sufferers imprisoned or isolated from society.

Ill-health assemblages reflect the physical, psychological and social relations that surround episodes of acute and chronic conditions. In an acute infection, there is a contagious ill-health assemblage: the infected body makes relations to others on behalf of the bacterium or virus, however much it tries not to do so. It has relations to the body that infected it, and so to all the bodies in the epidemic, and it stands in a one-to-many relation to all those it will infect. In neoplastic disease, there is an ill-health assemblage with relations to a myriad of health professions, to technologies and therapies, to life and death, and to (fear of) the future. In anorexia, the overwhelming relation is to food, and to a future slim body which has yet to come into existence, but which once attained will be free of pain and longing, gloriously released from the shackles of eating. What might be the key body relations in other ill-health assemblages, in conditions such as depression or multiple sclerosis?

The value of looking at ill-health as an assemblage is that it provides a holistic perspective on health and illness. Ill-health is a hugely complicated process, incorporating not only the biology of the disease, but also experiences, social and cultural factors, economics and even health policy. By counting and evaluating the intensity of the relations that a body has, it is possible to assess that body's limits, and what else it can do.

But this approach also recognizes that illness and health are not just things that happen to physical bodies. Rather, ill-health assemblages comprise networks, in which the physical body is just one element. The ill-health assemblage is a web of connections between bodies and their relations to physical, psychological and social elements, and our physical bodies are part of these wider networks. The overall impact of ill-health on an individual is a consequence of how all these relations interact together within the assemblage. But ill-health assemblages also affect the other elements, and may influence social organization, for instance of health care, of work expectations during the life course, and of the industries (for instance, agriculture and pharmaceuticals) that sustain our bodies in health. Bodies are the 'carriers' of health and illness, but the impacts of health and ill-health are far wider.

## The body and health

What, however, of the body in health? If there is an ill-health assemblage and a sickening-body, is there also a *health assemblage* and a becoming-healthy body? Can the approach to embodiment that looks at relations and how these are put together into assemblages help to make sense of the body (BwO) in health?

The answer to this latter question is yes, and indeed we already have the conceptual tools to make sense of the body in health. The relations that are in play during ill-health are mostly the same as those involved in the health assemblage; however, their intensities may be much attenuated or in some cases wholly absent. On the other hand, there may be other relations that are much stronger during good health: these once again may be physical, psychological, social and cultural, economic, political or philosophical.

However, the body is never passive, it always has capabilities, what else it can do. It follows that 'health' is not just an absence of disease relations (as suggested in the biomedical model), but a complex mix of all the different relations and forces along with the capacity of the body to make, resist and transform these relations (Buchanan 1997: 82). Friends, family and health professionals may be important within the mix of relations: they may tip the balance towards health by providing support and encouragement. The 'health' of a body is affected by

> . . . refracted and resisted relations, biological capabilities or cultural mind-sets, alliances with friends or health workers, struggles for control over treatment or conditions of living. Health is neither an absolute . . . to be aspired towards, nor an idealized outcome of 'mind-over-matter'. It is a process of becoming by (the body), of rallying relations, resisting physical or social territorialization, and experimenting with what is, and what it might become (Fox 2002a: 360)

Health (and ill-health) are thus not states, but processes, a becoming-other that fluctuates according to the intensity of relations that impinge on the body. They are opposing poles on a continuum, rather than alternative states of a body: the body (unless it is entirely moribund) always has some health left within it, and it would be exceptional for a body not to possess some elements of the ill-health assemblage. Rather than saying a body is healthy, we might talk about its 'becoming-healthy', or about the 'healthing' work of a body, to remind us of the active processes involved and the fluctuating nature of embodied health. This approach reminds us of the continually changing process of embodiment and the complex mix of relations that contribute to health.

It also has great relevance for health professionals as they care for and support people in health and illness. I described Deleuze and Guattari's model of embodiment in chapter 3, and discussed how bodies are territorialized by physical, psychological and social forces and how they can also be de-territorialized, and even achieve a 'line of flight' that will establish it within a new territory. Health and illness can be thought of as body *territories*, shaped by the ill-health or health assemblages. While some relations and forces may territorialize a body into ill-health (the *sickening* body), others may de-territorialize it. Relations to bacteria, poisons or pollutants territorialize the body into disease, and may need physical treatments or therapies to re-territorialize it to health. Others of the relations described earlier that contribute to the ill-health assemblage are psychological, social or economic. Relations with carers and family may be strengthened, to de-territorialize the sickening body away from the territory of illness, enhancing a line of flight of the body into a becoming-healthy body, even if this is only partial or temporary.

As an example, imagine how a knee replacement might open up new possibilities for Alice Martin, our osteoarthritic case study, or a bespoke wheelchair might provide a line of flight for a child with a condition such as cerebral palsy or spina bifida. But also, think how the support of a family member or a health professional might enhance the experiences of Alice or others with a chronic illness, either by material aid or just by offering encouragement or a friendly ear to share the problems of daily life (Bunting 1993: 14). What other elements of Alice's life might also open up the possibilities for what her body can do? And what may territorialize her further into ill-health? This dynamic model of health and illness provides the possibility that things can be different, that lines of flight can transform sick bodies, and that health professionals can be efficacious in this process. I will have more to say about this when we look at the body and care in chapter 7.

## The ageing body

We have identified the relations that create health and illness assemblages, and seen how these contribute to BwOs of the sickening body and the becoming-healthy body. Much ill-health in contemporary society is chronic rather than acute, and is often associated with disability and ageing. So it is appropriate to look briefly at relations and assemblages associated with ageing, some but not all of which are associated with health and illness.

Growing older cannot be reduced to the material effects of the passage of time on cells and organs. Time has psychological and cultural relations with bodies too, and the experience of ageing is diverse, and unique to the individual, because of the variation in body relations. In my study of older adults in Thailand and Australia (Fox 2005), 'old' people in Thailand were defined by the state (and themselves) as those over sixty, in contrast to Western culture, where old age begins much later, and 'sixty is the new forty'. The interviews I conducted showed the social and psychological relations of the ageing body in these different settings. Psychologically, ageing was tied to culture in many ways. For many of the Thai respondents, the experience of becoming older was associated with Buddhist beliefs.

> *Thai Mr O:* It is a good thing to be an old person, I feel good if there is someone to take care of me, and my body will go to the hospital after I die. It is a good way to live, I don't worry about life or about anything. It is the Buddhist philosophy: don't worry about anything, don't worry about your body, your life in the long run, I will give everything in the long run to the Government. . . . Religion is very important to me, to give respect to the Buddha, and do meditation every day. I am a very strict Buddhist.

For the Australians, there was no such overarching philosophy or world-view to bolster a sense of their humanity. Fatalism and a general stoicism seemed to structure how some of the older adults thought about their life.

> *Australian Mrs S:* I don't think about the future very much. We've just got to live a quiet life and we know quite a few of the people around. There are different things we can do. We

can read although I'm getting to the stage where I can't read, and that's a bit of a disappointment because I thought I would always be able to read. I think I live quite a dull life now, but the family are good.

The negative side of growing older is often associated with ill-health and infirmity, and the loss of capacities to act as they had done when younger. 'Keeping your health' was crucial, and it was perceived as something which had been 'taken away' as a result of getting older.

> *Australian Mrs C:* You think about old times, that's when you ask 'Why should it be me?' People at my age are still going like anything and I can't, that's what gets me down. You see people of 80 getting round, good as gold, not me. I've just got to put up with what I've got. If I could get around more, I wouldn't be here, not yet. . . . I live from day to day now.

Even when in relatively good physical fitness, the fear of future infirmity was sometimes a factor territorializing how the respondents thought about ageing.

> *Australian Mr L:* If you've got your health I guess it makes a difference. When I first came here I used to have a vegeta-ble garden growing down the side there. Emphysema gets progressively worse and there's nothing they can do for you. Well, I can't do the garden now so I've lost that interest. I would like to get involved in some of the other activities, like bowling, but I can't do that because I can't bend down. If your health goes, your spirit's gone.

The young often believe that ageing is implicitly negative, but this is not so. Both in Thailand and Australia, many of the people I spoke to were very positive about aspects of being older and of having fewer responsibilities. Perhaps for them, the character of relationships had changed, from the reciproc-ity of youth, to an acceptance of being a recipient. Unable to give anything back, they had somehow become more fulfilled in themselves.

> *Australian Mrs K:* I think ageing's all right. I don't mind it. You've all got to get old. You can't avoid it.

*Thai Mrs L:* I don't think about being old, in my mind I am still a school child because here we have everything, we have many activities. Where I live, it's just like a child who came to school. In the morning I come to the front of this home, and sing the national song, and at eight o'clock I go to the cafeteria here and at nine p.m. I go to bed.

For these older adults, age had brought all sorts of changes, not only in material life, but significantly, in how they understood themselves and their lives and biographies. Chronological age and the passage of time, economic and physical dependency, fear about the future, infirmity or incapacity: all were relations that contributed to the ageing assemblage. Sometimes, economic uncertainty could be the most territorializing aspect of growing older. For others, infirmity and the loss of freedom to do the simplest of activities were the most significant. On the other hand, even in the face of ontological challenges associated with death and impairment, some – notably the Buddhist Thais – found meaning and peace in the different phases of the life course. As one Thai said to me, 'it is good to be young, but it is also good to be old'. For each of these respondents, and for every body growing old, there is an assemblage deriving from the multitude of relations accrued over a lifetime. One such assemblage might be:

*The ageing assemblage no. 1*
The body has a relation to time: it passes time by holding on to, but eventually giving its capacities away, until there is nothing left to give, no more aspiration. It is engaged in giving up all that was once needed, saying 'I no longer have a use for this or that, what do I want with that any more?' It adopts new bodily strategies of self-care, risk reduction or perhaps abandonment. When the body is emptied of all it contained, it no longer aspires to anything.

Another assemblage might allow a line of flight for the body-without-organs:

*The ageing assemblage no. 2*
The body has a relation to time: time is the body's friend that allows a lifetime of experience to be celebrated. Each day brings new relations with family and friends and pleasure in the possibilities that life still offers as the body ages. As the body becomes more dependent it delights in the relations with family and carers.

What do you think is the message for health professionals here? How may they support ageing bodies to make the most of the possibilities, and to overcome the negatives that infirmity, dependency and insecurity might bring? How may they foster ageing assemblage 2 over ageing assemblage 1?

## Conclusion

In this chapter, I have explored the relations that affect bodies in terms of disease, illness and sickness, to show how these coalesce to establish ill-health and health assemblages. Health and illness are among the most significant aspects of embodiment during the life course, as these can have massive physical, psychological and emotional consequences for a body.

I have used the approach developed earlier in the book to show how both natural and cultural relations together shape health and illness bodies. Neither domain is predominant; both are critical to determining the forms of embodiment that are manifested during ill-health. Following Deleuze, Buchanan (1997: 82) described health as the 'actual measurable capacity to form new relations', and this is the formulation of health that I am working with here too. Health is quite clearly not the absence of disease, rather it is a de-territorialization of a body previously territorialized, perhaps by disease (the biomedical factor), illness (the experience of ill-health) and sickness (the cultural response to being ill). Health is a line of flight out of these conditions, made possible by changes in the quantity and intensity of certain relations, and the body's capacity to become-other, to be creative about itself.

Within this perspective, assemblages that consume the body lead to disintegration, while those that enhance the body's capacities, which de-territorialize and allow lines of flight, lead to health. The quick look at ageing bodies suggested the possibilities for de-territorialization and a line of flight. Despite the territorialization of ageing; the effects of loss of function or the depredations of poverty or social isolation, ageing bodies can still become-other, finding new meaning in the experience of ageing.

So 'health' is – at least in part – the *resistance* of the body to territorialization. Resistance is not only a possibility: it is the character of an active, creative body-self that refracts the relations which impinge upon it. Health is not a state of physical well-being, nor is it really about the physical body. Rather it is a process of becoming by the body, of rallying relations, resisting physical or social territorialization, and experimenting with what is, and what might become (Fox 2002a). Health is an assemblage that links the body into its physical, social and cultural environment, and offers new possibilities for what else a body can do. Health professionals play a key role not only in treating disease, but as key components within the health assemblage, as we will see in more detail when we look at the body and care in chapter 7.

### Suggested further reading

Fox, N. J. (2005) Cultures of ageing in Thailand and Australia (what can an ageing body do?) *Sociology*, 39 (3), 501–18.

Freund, P. E. S., McGuire, M. B. and Podhurst, L. S. (2003) *Health, Illness and the Social Body*. Upper Saddle River, NJ: Prentice Hall.

Kleinman, A., Eisenberg, L. and Good, B. (2006) Culture, illness, and care: clinical lessons from anthropologic and cross-cultural research. *Focus: The Journal of Lifelong Learning in Psychiatry*, 4 (1), 140–9.

# CHAPTER FIVE

# Desire and the Body

Having desires goes hand in hand with possessing a body. Some, such as hunger or thirst, seem driven by biological forces we can do little to control. Even the most unworldly of individuals: a religious hermit for instance, will experience an urge for food or water, however much they try to banish such bodily needs from their consciousness. Other desires, from sexual attraction to consumer wishes, are less driven by our physiology and can be partially or fully controlled, managed or repressed by our conscious efforts. It's unlikely that an hour goes by without some desire surfacing in our minds: from urges to eat, drink or gain sexual fulfilment, to desire for academic, sporting or other personal success or satisfaction.

Some desires are accompanied by physical responses (salivation, sexual arousal), others are not. Our appetites and desires play a part in structuring our waking lives, just as they do for any living creature. The body's need for nourishment and a safe living space; the desire for sexual stimulation and release; our urges to buy a new designer outfit, a new car, the latest gadget or our favourite music download; and our desires and wishes for ourselves and our futures, all affect not only our thoughts and feelings, but also how we are motivated to act on a daily basis.

Desire can be short-term or last for a lifetime. Our lives may be more or less dominated by a mission to achieve this or that: a career, money, a partner, the perfect figure, success as an artist or a performer. Daily life can indeed become fixated on an unfulfilled desire: perhaps this is a feature of the human condition? Certainly our cultures and economies have recognized this fact: in a 'consumer society', the human capacity for desire has been exploited mercilessly. Vast malls of shopping outlets pander to our mainstream desires, while less conspicuous suppliers can provide goods or services to meet unconventional or more private desires, for instance for sexual gratification, mind-altering drugs, or even delicacies such as rare vintages of wine or uncommon foodstuffs. The Internet has globalized the marketplace, bringing together desire and supply to service any conceivable appetite. Think for a moment about your own consumer desires and how you have fulfilled them recently.

This chapter will look at the desiring body: the body that is driven to change itself by the acquisition of its 'object of desire', or by the very creative, productive forces that drive it to become – in one way or another – different from what it currently is. Once again, I will use an approach that accepts the body as both natural and social, by exploring the physical, psychological and cultural relations that affect the body's desiring. I will explore two of the principal focuses of the desiring body: sexuality and the consumption of food (and its influence on body size and shape). With insights from these areas, I will explore desire more broadly, looking at the creative body, and the ways in which desiring bodies shape the world.

## The object of desire

Anything can become the object (or focus) of a human being's desire, in the sense that humans seem to have a limitless capacity to target their attention, their wishes, their aspirations to possess or control any object. This object could be a rare stamp, a missing piece of a jigsaw (literal or metaphorical), a pair of shoes, a new kitchen, a pet cat or dog and, of course, another human being (as a friend, a sexual partner, an employee or whatever). Desire has motivated the great events of history and the dramas of literature. Aspiring rulers have sought a kingdom, politicians to govern. Julius Caesar desired an empire that reached to the edges of the world; Hitler desired German 'living space' (*lebensraum*) that led him to invade much of Western Europe. Commercially, corporations have desired to dominate a market. Thieves desire objects owned by others that they wish to possess, without the inconvenience of having to pay for them.

Objects of desire may be physical or abstract. A musician may aspire to be 'the best', and accolades or prizes are secondary to that knowledge of excellence. A student may desire knowledge of her subject, to achieve mastery over it. In Christopher Marlowe's play *Dr Faustus*, the title character goes to extremes: he trades his soul to accomplish his desire for worldly knowledge and pleasure. This concept of 'mastery' is often associated with objects of desire: ideas of possession, control, ownership, are all aspects of how we imagine things will be once we have acquired our object of desire. We are defined (territorialized) by a *lack* prior to acquiring this object of desire, while we may re-define (re-territorialize) ourselves in terms of 'mastery' once the object is in our grasp.

Historically speaking, human cultures have often concerned themselves with deciding which objects of desire are legitimate. In the Judaeo-Christian tradition, we are told not to 'covet (desire) our neighbour's ox, or their husband or wife'. Laws prohibit acting on some desires: theft is prohibited, as are other strategies to acquire wealth such as fraud or tax evasion. Sex is a focus for a range of taboos and laws: objects of sexual desire may not include close blood relatives; those beneath the 'age of consent' (variously 12, 14, 16, 18 and 21 years old, at different times in history); animals; and in some cultures, same-sex contacts and married people. In racist regimes (such as the early twentieth-century US or apartheid South Africa), inter-racial sexual contacts and marriage ('miscegenation') were also forbidden. Sexual objects of desire other than the conventional erotic zones of consenting adults (for instance, bondage practices or fetish objects such as high-heeled shoes) have been defined as 'perversions' or deviancies from 'normal' sexual practice. Foodstuffs are similarly hedged with prohibi-tions: Jews and Moslems should not desire pork; dairy and meat cannot be eaten in the same meal by Jews; while veg-etarians may feel guilt if they have urges to eat meat (Douglas 1966: 41ff.). Needless to say, laws, prohibitions and taboos do not preclude desires, though they may control or prevent people acting upon them.

The psychiatrist Sigmund Freud was one of the first theo-rists of desire. His theory and method of 'psychoanalysis' was built upon a view that sexual desire emerges and is structured during the early years of life, even from birth as the infant suckles at its mother's breast. I will look at Freud's model more closely later in this chapter, so for now it will suffice to say that, for Freud, 'normal' sexual development (meaning a focus on an adult member of the opposite sex as the object of desire) could be achieved only if various stages of infantile desire were first successfully navigated. Children, according to Freud (1973: 118–21), focus initially upon themselves and their parents as objects of desire, and struggle through an 'Oedipal' phase (in which they desire to possess their opposite sex parent) before emerging during adolescence into the adult form of desire 'proper' to their gender, namely another adult of the opposite sex.

This very crude psychoanalytic model of sexual desire was greatly elaborated and refined during the last century to over-come its obvious weaknesses and inherent heterosexism, but has also been the subject of criticism from very many quarters, including scientific psychology and psychiatry, feminism and sociology. Among these critics were Deleuze and Guattari, whose approach we have already encountered in this book. Their first collaboration was actually entitled *Anti-Oedipus* (Deleuze and Guattari 1984). They rejected psychoanalysis because it suggested that the key to mental health lay with the individual and the nuclear family in which a child grows up. In contrast, Deleuze and Guattari considered that the real source of unhappiness and mental ill-health was the wider (capitalist) society in which contemporary people live. Our society, they argued, had created a proliferating supply of commodities to endlessly fuel a desire that could never be satisfied.

However, Deleuze and Guattari also had a more fundamental criticism of this psychoanalytic approach to understanding the body and its desires. Freud's approach, they said, used a model of desire that had dominated Western ideas of the body since the ancient Greek philosopher Plato. Desire, in this view, was a gap, lack or void waiting to be filled by the *acquisition* of the object that is desired. But this kind of desire is always doomed to be unfulfilled, because our fantasy object of desire is unattainable: reality will always fall short of our fantasies (Bogue 1989: 89). Thus, for instance, sexual desire might focus on a fantasy object (such as might be seen in a magazine, online, or simply in our imagination) which reality can never match, while our purchase of a new pair of shoes or the latest mobile phone will similarly never be as good as the fantasy ones we desired.

The trouble with this way of thinking about desire, say Deleuze and Guattari, is that it emphasizes fantastical objects of desire, and guarantees disappointment (Deleuze and Guattari 1984: 25). This attachment to fantasy objects (the image of the perfect naked body or the little black dress that will help you look 10 pounds slimmer) creates dependency or a 'slave mentality' (Butler 1990), which undermines the capacity of humans to act in the world, to change it and themselves.

Deleuze and Guattari argued that this depressing prospect (which is the conclusion of most theories of desire) ignores the primary, motivating force of desire itself, which is not about acquisition at all. Instead, they wanted to emphasize the *productive* aspect of desire, which is the creative life-force itself. The productive process of desiring is the motivating, creative energy that enables people to actually shed attachments to the latest fashion or the norms of social conduct, to become something more, something else, someone freed from a sense of lacking an object or another person. To reiterate a phrase already familiar to readers of this book: productive desire can enable people to realize what *else* a body can do.

Deleuze and Guattari saw productive or positive desire as the motivator for all human action in the world. It goes far beyond desire for food, or sexual gratification, or consumer goods. Desire is what inspires every action, from providing care to a patient, to painting a portrait, to cooking the supper, to studying for a degree. It is all the '. . . ing' processes that we do: the desiring body is the motivated, 'doing' body. Think about your own motivations: meeting friends for pleasure, making a tasty meal, reading this book to gain knowledge or pass a test: all are examples of your productive desire, which together comprise living in the world. Our culture has over-emphasized the 'object of desire' and ignored the *subject* of desire, the motivated, creative body itself.

It is with this dual understanding of desire, as both a lack that can limit an individual to craving for the newest fad, a hotter sexual partner or the next drink, and as a productive force that motivates and enables, that I will now look at the desiring body, and what it can do, looking first at sexual desire, and then exploring desire more widely in relation to consumption, and more specifically, the consumption of food.

## Sexuality and the desiring body

Sexuality is one of the most discussed and theorized of all the body's desires, with a range of theories developed by biological and social scientists to explain it. Most, at some point, make links to the biological and social attributes of the body known as 'sex' and 'gender' respectively. The former is based upon a biological definition of bodies into male and female (sexual dimorphism), while gender refers to the experience of being male or female, and of society's responses to matters of sexual identity.

From a biological perspective, human sexual dimorphism derives ultimately from genetic differences, along with environment factors (for instance, exposure to androgenic or oestrogenic chemicals prenatally or in adulthood). Genes and hormones influence sexual development from the earliest stages of embryonic growth, and continue as humans grow, undergo puberty and mature into adults (Hines 2006). Sexuality is considered to be a direct result of the 'sexualized' tissues and organs that are expressed by these genetic and biochemical determinants, and mediate the sexual capacities of the body to mate and to reproduce. Recent research suggests there is actually a continuum between male and female, with bodies situated somewhere along this continuum, toward one or other pole. All bodies produce androgens (male hormones) and oestrogens (female hormones) regardless of their sex, and the relative levels of these may affect both physical characteristics (for instance, distribution of body hair, shape of vocal cords, and muscle bulk) and behaviour (androgens seem to predispose bodies to more aggressive or dominant action) (Sapolsky 1998). Sexuality may be a consequence, in this theory, of the balance of hormones circulating in the bloodstream. However, evidence of this is patchy: levels of prenatal testosterone, for example, seem to influence some behaviours, but not gender identity or sexual preferences (Hines 2006: 155).

Social science and feminist theories tend to approach sexuality by focusing on the experiential aspects of gender, sexual identity and sexual differences, and upon cultural attitudes to male and female bodies. These theories expose the 'social construction' not only of bodies but also of their behaviour, including sexual behaviour and sexuality. In the past, men's sexuality was seen as normal and unproblematic, while women's sexuality was regarded as uncontrollable, wild and dangerous. Extreme examples of how patriarchal control of female sexuality was manifested included the murder of 'witches' who challenged social order, and the genital mutilation of women in whom sexual arousal was to be eradicated or minimized. Both masculine and feminine sexualities have been shown to be changing, breaking free from stereotypes and social expectations (Bernasconi 2010: 872; McCormack and Anderson 2010: 855). These social theories often dispute any 'natural' basis for sexuality, regarding sexual behaviour as a consequence of social attitudes and norms.

Neither a strict biological nor a strict social model of sexuality satisfactorily can capture the dual character of sexual desire as both embodied and physical, and socially constructed and context-specific. Various theories have sought to bring these aspects of sexuality together. In the modern period, Freud was the first to attempt to explain the processes that underpin sexual desire. For Freud, there was a dynamic between an innate (and unconscious) biological drive that he called the 'libido', that motivates humans towards their objects of desire, and the socially constructed meanings applied to people or things that determine what becomes an object of desire.

Freud sought to explain how adult sexuality developed in apparently asexual children, both in its 'natural' form (which for Freud and his contemporaries meant a heterosexual desire consummated in an adult relationship) and in deviations from this norm, including so-called 'perversions' or other 'unnatural' manifestations. He offered the remarkable proposition (for its time) that children were sexual from birth, but that infantile sexuality was naturally focused on the parents and on aspects of the child's own bodily processes such as suckling at the breast and excretion, and that only by successful transitions through these phases would an adult, genital sexuality (focused on the opposite sex) emerge following puberty (Freud 1973: 118). For a boy child, the 'Oedipus' conflict made the mother the object of desire, while the father was a rival suitor for her affection (Freud 1973: 118–21). A similar 'Electra' complex affected girl children. If the child works 'successfully' through these conflicts, he or she might emerge into normal (heterosexual) adulthood. However, if 'Oedipalization' did not 'take' successfully (Bogue 1989: 89), the objects of desire would remain immature, which might lead to neurosis during adulthood. Thus, for example, Freud considered that a liking for oral sex in adulthood demonstrated an incomplete (and thus unsuccessful) passage through the earliest oral fixations of infants at their mother's breast!

Freud's theories have been broadly discounted as unscientific and sexist, and based on the unfounded belief that heterosexuality is the natural manifestation of human sexuality. For Freud, homosexuality, bisexuality, taking pleasure in oral sex or fetish objects (non-sexual objects such as latex garments or high-heeled shoes that for some people are associated with sexual arousal) all reflected problems that occurred in the early years of life. Freudian approaches ignore a far wider social context that impinges on human bodies and may influence the direction of the sexual drive. For Gagnon and Simon (2005), human sexuality develops exclusively within a social context, and it is the socially constructed meanings of the body and other objects in its environment that determine

> ... the ways in which the physical activities of sex are learned, and the ways in which these activities are integrated into larger social scripts and social arrangements where meaning and sexual behaviour come together to create sexual conduct. (Gagnon and Simon 2005: 5)

They argue that sexual activity is the outcome of a 'vast array' of learnt responses to physiological, psychological and social elements, which together establish 'scripts' within which sexuality is played out: 'the very experience of sexual excitement that seems to originate from hidden internal sources is in fact a learned response' (ibid.: 9). Think, for example, of the rituals surrounding dating, including pre-date preening and display, a night out at the movies or a restaurant, alcohol consumption, and tentative or not-so-tentative sexual explorations. These activities situate sexual desire within an established social formation, in which sex becomes familiar and predictable.

This approach sees sexuality as almost entirely a social process, with little relation to biology. Sexuality is progressively learnt during development, and consequently is highly fluid: leading to a wide diversity of possible sexualities. The value of such an approach is to emphasize the importance of the everyday social contexts within which bodies engage in sexual activity (Jackson and Scott 2010: 823), in contrast to theories that focus upon early childhood development.

Another important approach that focused predominantly upon the social processes that affect bodies' sexual expression derived from Foucault's *History of Sexuality*, an unfinished series of studies (1984, 1985, 1986) that was cut short by the author's death. Foucault sought to show how throughout history, bodies, pleasure and sexuality have become the focus for systematic 'discourses' (socially accepted arguments), which provide authoritative statements and norms about how humans should behave sexually. In this reading, social norms and values entirely govern how bodies should behave. Sexuality was not, Foucault argued, some kind of biological drive. Rather it was a blueprint for relations between bodies: male and female, young and old, parents and children, professionals and laity (Foucault 1984: 103). At different points in history, sexual desire and sexual pleasure were channelled by these discourses on sexual behaviour, to create specific sexualities (modes of sexual expression) in people and bodies. Thus, being 'heterosexual' or 'homosexual' are sexual identities that have become possible for us because the current dominant discourses on sexuality set these out as the only options.

Looking back in history, Foucault showed how statements about sexuality became important texts that formed an era's 'body of knowledge' about sexual conduct. Discourse was applied to bodies and their desires and relations to other bodies, to create frameworks for sexuality. At different points in time, these discourses would shape the sexual body, establishing a 'regime of truth' about sexual matters that seemed absolute. Thus in pre-Christian Greece, bisexuality and paedophilia were a 'normal' part of civilized sexual life, in which older men would have love affairs with teenage boys, while using their wives for child-rearing and household management (Foucault 1985: 187ff.). In later Roman and Greek societies, sex carried with it medical and moral risks and had to be moderated and managed carefully (Foucault 1986: 97ff.).

Foucault described four discourses on sexual bodies that emerged from the eighteenth century onwards: the recognition of the female body as 'saturated with sexuality' and thus prone to psychiatric disorder; the discovery of an immature sexuality in children that must be regulated (the basis for Freud's later theory); a focus on the economic and political consequences of reproduction for society and thus for parents; and the view that sexual instincts were separate from other biological or psychological drives (Foucault 1984: 103–5). These feel very modern: together these have contributed to the shape that sexuality takes in the century leading to the present.

Discourses on sexuality have tended to extend further and further into society over time: the early perspectives were aimed at the ruling classes of ancient Greece and Rome, whereas in the past two centuries, sexual discourses have succeeded in establishing themselves throughout all classes of society (Foucault 1984: 121). Foucault did not see the most recent history of sexual behaviour as a progressive liberation of human bodies from the constraints of nineteenth-century repression into a free-for-all. What appears to be a more 'liberated' expression of sexuality in contemporary society, he argued, was the emergence of a new discourse on what bodies are, and how they should behave, in which every aspect of sexuality was to be opened to observation, dissection and confession (Foucault 1984: 130–1). Think of all the meticulous discussions of every aspect of our sexuality today, from psychoanalysis and sex therapy to endless TV programmes and magazine quizzes about how to have better sex. Sex has been turned into a new focus for anxiety: am I giving my partner good orgasms; are my body and body parts the right size and shape?

In feminism and queer theory (a subversive approach that challenges traditional heterosexist assumptions), sexuality has been recognized as important for how identities are forged and sustained. Research by Scharff (2010) found that a strong female or male identity may depend upon a commitment to heterosexuality, while other sexualities blur or problematize gender identities. Butler (1990: 135, 139) takes the view that how we act sexually and who we desire: these 'performances' of sexuality and gender, establish our identities and sexualities. There is no absolute biological foundation to sex, gender or sexuality: our sexuality is shaped by our actions alone (ibid.: 31).

These theories of sexual desire contribute insights into the role of biology and social forces, with varying emphases, ranging from Freud's conflict between a purely animal sex drive and the civilizing influences of culture, to Butler's conclusion that sexuality is entirely detached from the biology of the body. The Deleuzian model used in this book proceeds rather differently, acknowledging the range of biological, psychological and social body-relations involved in a 'sexuality assemblage'. A body is shaped into a sexuality by influences that include biology and culture, which influence how the productive sexual desire of the body is directed.

In this approach, disparate relations and affects contribute to the shape of a body's sexual response and its sexuality. The biological relations that affect sex and sexuality include the body's genetic and physiological make-up: chromosomes, sex hormones associated with reproduction and sexual arousal and gratification, and the anatomical and physiological attributes of the body that derive from these. The body may also be affected by physical sensations (touch, sight, smell, taste) that lead to arousal, and also by the voluntary and involuntary nervous processes that lead to sexual gratification.

A sexual body's psychological and emotional relations are established from infancy onwards, though less through the kinds of mechanisms that Freud proposed, and more through the experiences of physical and psychological intimacy (and its absence) that may occur in interactions with family, friends and lovers. Positive feelings of sexual pleasure, engagement and confidence, and negative feelings of sexual inadequacy, guilt, anxiety, fear or disgust concerning sex may all emerge from the relations built up during childhood and adult life. Strong emotions may come to be associated with matters sexual: from love for a sexual partner to jealousy or anger at another's sexual conduct. Sexual experiences will bolster or inhibit these positive and negative feelings.

Cultural contexts supply the social relations within which sex, gender and sexuality are performed. Sex and gender stereotypes, social judgements about sexual behaviour, norms of attractiveness and what counts as 'erotic', moral and religious constraints and the economic and political forces that sustain gender differences and inequalities all contribute relations that will contribute to the sexuality assemblage. The discourses that Foucault described (look back now, to remind yourself of these) are part of this cultural context. Concepts such as 'love', 'marriage', 'monogamy', 'sexual liberation', 'virginity' and so forth will also affect the desiring body. For example, previous generations may have been influenced by an ethics of conformity to public morality, whereas today, a need for 'authenticity' (being 'true to oneself') provides the foundation for sexual conduct and sexuality (Bernasconi 2010: 873).

My approach does not reduce sexuality to either its biological drive, or to the social and cultural contexts, as do some other theories reviewed earlier. Sexuality is influenced by a vast range of relations, some biological and some social in character, some powerful, others weak. Some of these are common to everyone in a culture (for instance, most people in Western cultures try to avoid being naked in public), while others are individual, deriving from personal experiences. Reflect for a moment on your own experiences, and how these may have influenced your sexual conduct and sexual identity.

Together, these myriad relations affect what a sexual body can do, and what else it can do. Importantly, however, these relations interact to create assemblages, which establish the *limits* for the positive desire or drive of the body. *Sexuality is not the drive itself: rather it is the territorialization of the body.* However, this territorialization is unstable and always subject to new relations; open to a 'line of flight' that can allow the sexual body to become other. Interestingly, this would suggest that there are no boundaries to sexuality, but that human sexuality is typically highly constrained and unimaginative, limited in its creativity by an assemblage comprising all the biological, psychological and social relations that impinge on the sexual body.

This analysis of sexual desire offers insights relevant to everybody's lives, but it also has specific implications for health care professionals. Patients' sexuality has often been ignored or denied when it comes to providing care (sometimes even when medical conditions are concerned with sexual function). Sex seems to have no place in a professionalized care setting. Sexual desire is discounted as a component of the body, almost as if a person's sexuality has been left at the door when they enter a clinic or hospital. Old people, in particular, have been considered as asexual (Gott 2006), and their sexuality, if manifested, considered as a 'problem' to be suppressed in the care setting. We have avoided so far in this text any mention of our case study Alice Martin's sexuality, as if because she is 75, sexuality is irrelevant. Yet Alice will have had a full and hopefully satisfying sex life with her husband, and perhaps she is still driven from time to time by sexual desire. The loss of sexual drive, or the loss of opportunities to express sexuality in a youth-oriented society, can be a tragedy for older people who may feel a part of them has been forcibly removed from them as they aged (Gott and Hinchliff 2003; Steinke 1994). By recognizing that desire is a feature of embodiment, carers can acknowledge this aspect of patients' bodies, and integrate care that takes sexual desire into account. On the other hand, sexuality can become a problem in caring. Indeed, sexual contacts between doctors and patients are explicitly prohibited under law, although desire does not somehow evaporate in such contexts. Care settings may be managed to de-sexualize the body, for instance during intimate examinations (Emerson 1970), but this should be done in collaboration with patients, to help both parties feel comfortable with forced intimacy.

## Consumption, food and the eating-body

As we have seen in relation to sexual desire, desiring is a feature of embodiment that links the body's natural and social aspects. I have suggested that desire, in the Deleuzian sense, is itself the creative, active principle that motivates human bodies. As such, it links directly to the biological capacities of living bodies to grow, actively make choices that determine their lives on a minute-to-minute basis, and more long-term, and engage productively with the world around them. At the same time, bodies may focus on *objects* of desire, which can be inanimate or animate, physical, psychological or abstract. The choice of an object of desire, I have argued in the context of sexuality, is determined by assemblages of relations deriving from biology, psychology and culture.

Together, the motivating desire of the body and the object of desire shaped by body assemblages can provide a way to understand consumption in all its diversity, from the ingestion of food and drink in order to physically survive, through to the excesses of consumerism that have filled our shopping malls and warehouses with the consumer goods of an affluent society. Even the over-consumption of the world's environment and its resources are open to this kind of analysis. I will focus here on one specific connection between desire and consumption: eating, and how this desire can become disordered.

In chapter 3, I used the example of eating, and specifically eating a vegetarian diet, to illustrate the assemblages of biological, psychological and cultural relations that determine a body's eating. Thus, while a newborn's food-desiring assemblage may comprise simply:

>hunger – mouth – food,

it is quickly elaborated into

>hunger – mouth – food – nipple – mother

and so forth, as a child is weaned and develops its own tastes. For the adult, the eating assemblage might comprise:

>hunger – mouth – food – appetite – tastes – money – shopping – dietary choices – time

along with many other relations particular to the context and experiences of the individual.

Desiring and consuming food are clearly influenced both by the physical need to satisfy hunger and sustain life, and by psychologically and culturally influenced choices over what to eat: appetites and tastes. We are all affected by these each time we choose food to eat, but the relations become most evident where there is an over-arching structure for diet. Vegetarians make such choices every day, at each mealtime, based not only on appetites but also upon a principle: their eating assemblages incorporate relations to abstract ideas such as animal welfare. They may physically desire to eat bacon or chicken, but end up replacing these objects of desire with vegetarian alternatives. Health, environment and animal rights may all be factors determining vegetarians' food choices, with health and ethics as the main reasons cited by vegetarians for their diets. Over time, however, those already vegetarian sometimes develop additional environmental reasons for avoiding meat (which is much more harmful to the environment than plant foodstuffs). This relation with ideas of ecology and sustainable living contributes further to a vegetarian-eating assemblage that sustained food choice from meal to meal (Fox and Ward 2008c, 2008d).

Whether diet is structured by vegetarianism or simply by preferences, economic constraints, availability of foodstuffs or commercial interests (processed foods may be promoted over raw foodstuffs, for instance), once again we can see a variety of relations that together create the eating assemblages that govern food ingestion. This can be of use, for example, when trying to improve the diet of an elderly person or an infant, or change the eating habits of a population.

To understand the ways in which desire can impact on health, I want to look at two conditions of 'disordered eating' affecting contemporary society: obesity and anorexia. In both, the desiring body has relations that have established limits on what an eating-body can do, patterning eating to an extent which results in over- or under-weight. Let us look at the eating assemblages of relations to make sense of these conditions and how they can be treated.

For 'obesity' (a medically defined level of over-weight), important relations may be physical (a gene predisposing to high body mass index or an endocrine disorder such as hypothyroidism; or it may be psychological relations that have made over-eating habitual, or a source of comfort or security. Cultural relations could also play a part: in some cultures, over-weight is desirable and a sign of affluence or well-being. The outcome of the eating assemblage in this case is that food intake exceeds that required for sustenance, as the body fails to gain fulfilment from its object of desire. Therapy may entail deconstructing the eating assemblage, to understand which relations (biological or social) have become so powerful that the body's desire has lost touch with its physical needs or its capacity for balance.

Theories of anorexia suggest a range of factors that may cause the condition (Fox et al. 2005b: 946), ranging again from biological to cultural. Although there are some biological bases for anorexia, many theorists argue that anorexia is actually a strategy for gaining control over life: by managing the body's shape through diet, people suffering from anorexia seek to achieve control in an otherwise chaotic life. Within the 'pro-anorexia' movement (which supports those trying to live out an anorectic lifestyle), the community fosters relations that celebrate and promote a very low body weight, sometimes using drugs aimed at overweight people. Pro-anorexia websites publish tips and tricks to control calorie intake, but also use images of skinny celebrity bodies as 'thinspiration', bolstering anorectic assemblages with further relations to thin (Fox et al. 2005b: 960). Here the eating assemblage would include:

> food – hunger – body shape – problems – control – proana community – thinspiration – weight-loss drugs.

In anorexia, the object of desire is no longer food itself, but the skinny body that is the objective of fasting. Buchanan (1997: 78) argues that the anorexic patient seeks to 'liberate the body' from the burden of a biological urge to eat: the anorexia assemblage draws on psychological and cultural relations to drown out the temptations of food. Eventually, anorexia becomes a limit on what the body can do, because food is no longer seen as positive or nutritious, but an evil to be denied. Therapy for anorexia, as with other disordered eating-bodies, needs to explore individuals' eating assemblages, which have resulted in this limit on what the eating body can do. By changing the 'myriad of cognitive, emotional, cultural, social and philosophical relations' (Fox and Ward 2008c: 2592) that comprise the anorexia assemblage (some of which may have little or no direct connection to food consumption), the assemblage may be de-territorialized, and the body achieve a line of flight out of its anorectic state. Needless to say, this may be a complex and lengthy therapeutic process, involving working through painful experiences and associations to unpack the assemblage that has led to a disorder of desiring.

I focused in this section upon eating and some of its disorders, but as I noted earlier, this kind of approach can be applied to every aspect of consumption, every object of desire that is the focus for human longing. In today's world, we have been surrounded by consumer goods and services that marketing and advertising seek to make desirable. For many people, the only relation in their consumption assemblage preventing an orgy of indulgence is an economic one, although beliefs (for

instance, in moderation, anti-materialism or sustainable consumption) may also limit consuming bodies. All our bodies
are shaped by this consumption assemblage which is backed
by powerful economic and industrial interests. I leave it to you
to reflect on what that means for bodies in today's consumer
society.

## Desire and creativity

In this chapter, we have looked at two areas of desire that
have consequences for the human race and its continuity, and
for individuals. For both sexuality and eating assemblages,
we have seen the body's interactions with relations that are
both biological and social. In each, even where drives such as
hunger or sexual arousal motivate desire, psychology and culture may win out, to focus sexual desire or to manage body
shape through food consumption. In each case, we have
explored the inter-relationship between the motivated desire
of the body and the objects it desires. I began the chapter by
suggesting that theories of desire have focused on objects of
desire at the expense of understanding the desiring body itself.
I want to end the chapter by standing back from objects of
desire entirely, to look more closely at the part that the motivated desiring body plays in the body's capacity for creative,
productive action. I will suggest that this provides an angle on
human behaviour in general, and health behaviour and risk in
particular.

Creativity has seemed a difficult concept for psychology and
the other social sciences to pin down, often struggling with
conceptions of novelty and inherent value, or focusing on
the circumstances under which creativity occurs, particularly
when considering artistic creation (Ford 1996). Innovation
can cover many aspects of life, from technology to management to cookery, and studies have suggested that some people
are more effective than others at innovating (Kirton 1994).

From a Deleuzian perspective, creativity is not something

restricted to the outputs of artists, engineers, philosophers or entrepreneurs. Rather, it is the moment-to-moment 'becoming-other' of the motivated body, as it acts in and upon the world around it. Desire, the positive motivation that ceaselessly drives human action in endless choice-making and interaction with others, is the productive process that creates not only works of art and scientific inventions, but the day-to-day organization of bodies and things in time and space. Non-human animals act in very limited ways on objects in their environment: consuming them, marking them territorially, mating with them and reproducing, perhaps chasing and killing other animals. Humans, through their capacity to use tools and develop technology, have far more potential for creative production, and many of their creative outputs are social or abstract in character, from establishing a family unit to generating ideas or models of the world in science, engineering or philosophy. The dynamic mix of motivated desire, and the sheer number and diversity of bodies' relations, means endless possibilities for creative production.

Let me illustrate this approach by looking again at Alice Martin, the older adult we met earlier in the book, and her first consultation with a health care professional concerning the onset of osteoarthritis. We join the consultation as Alice enters: she has never met this professional previously. The professional invites Alice to sit, and asks some questions, beginning with a general enquiry about health, and moving on to symptoms. As Alice tells her story, the professional asks further questions, trying to develop a working theory of what may be the problem. Having heard about symptoms, the professional examines Alice physically and takes some measurements: pulse rate, blood pressure. She then offers a diagnosis of age-related osteoarthritis, and Alice and the professional discuss this, the need for further tests and possible treatment outcomes.

This routine meeting, like so many which occur countless times in clinics throughout the world, is produced entirely through the interactions of Alice's and the professional's bodies, though many biological, psychological and social relations play a part in the production of this 'consultation'. It was more or less successful; at least from the professional's point of view, as it achieved objectives of diagnosis and disease management planning. Her desire, and Alice's, drove the meeting forward from introductions through to conclusion, as decisions were made, ideas were tested and agreed, discussions and physical activities were enacted, towards a goal that was at least partly shared by Alice and the professional.

During the consultation, the active, motivated desires of the two participants were channelled and constrained by the relations that mediate their embodiment. For the professional, cultural norms concerning her role as an expert and a carer, her knowledge of biomedicine, and her status and authority to diagnose and control clinical resources were important relations. For Alice, her knowledge of her body and her expectations of care, but also her fear and anxiety, her social and economic position and her past experiences of medicine and care contributed. While the other human being in the encounter provided an important relation in determining the outcome for Alice, many, many other relations also played a part.

This one small element of daily life illustrates the part that desire plays in creating the world on a minute-to-minute basis, as bodies act on things and other bodies, affecting physically or socially. It recognizes the active part humans play in producing the world through their motivated desire, but also the essential part that body relations have in constraining what bodies can do. The limits relations (within assemblages) impose on bodies create the regularities and predictability of social life. Yet every moment of the day, human desire also produces novelty and unexpected outcomes. Relations, and the assemblages they constitute, are not all-determining: the creativity inherent in productive desire can take a body in an unexpected direction, in the process adding to the richness and diversity of daily life.

I chose a mundane example to show human desire in action, but we can also apply this model to creative acts of musical or artistic composition, or scientific or technological innovation (Deleuze and Guattari 1988: 493). Such creations are different only in quality from the daily creations of a conversation between friends or a particularly tasty meal. The great acts of creativity still reflect only a body's desire, a de-territorialization of an assemblage, and a re-territorialization that affects the world in some significant way. The discovery of penicillin, the painting of Van Gogh's *Sunflowers* or the conclusion that $E = MC2$ are remarkable only in the breadth of their subsequent influence: for a short while desire allows a body to 'speak the truth' to others, be that an artistic, a literary or a scientific truth. The history of human culture, from the mundane social production of all our lives through to the great steps in civilization and enlightenment, may be understood in this perspective as the outpouring of embodied desiring, shaped by assemblages of physical, psychological and cultural relations.

In this chapter I have shown how desire is not only an underpinning drive within the body, but also a motivating energy that leads to creativity and social production. Sexuality, consumption and creativity are all consequences of motivation and assemblages. Desire is fundamental to embodiment, and intertwined with our life course, growth and maturation, health, illness and ageing processes. Desiring – this motivating, creative drive – is synonymous with life itself: only with our last gasp does desire finally fade away. However, as we shall see in the next chapter, this core element of embodiment – desire – has also meant that the body has become a problem to be managed.

### Suggested further reading

Foucault, M. (1984) *The History of Sexuality Vol. 1: The Will to Knowledge.* Harmondsworth: Penguin.

Freud, S. (1973) *New Introductory Lectures on Psychoanalysis.* Harmondsworth: Penguin.

Gagnon, J. H. and Simon, W. (2005) *Sexual Conduct: the Social Sources of Human Sexuality.* Piscataway, NJ: Transaction Publishers.

# CHAPTER SIX

# The Managed Body

In the last chapter, I looked at how desire is the body's motivation for action, either directed toward an object of desire (for example, a new dress, the latest phone or a person), or to affect the world creatively and productively. This capacity for bodies to affect things and other bodies, physically and socially, drives the dynamic, unpredictable unfolding of daily life. Bodies, shaped by assemblages of connections to other bodies, things and ideas, may also themselves change, 'becoming' different as they interact with the physical and social environment. It would be wrong, however, to imagine that there is a free-for-all, in which this capacity for bodies to change (and to change the world around them) happens without constraints, organization and order.

Actually, bodies are limited in how they act and affect the world around them in all sorts of ways, from the effects of gravity and the passage of time through to political and legal regulation of bodies. Back in chapter 3, we looked in detail at the different kinds of physical, psychological and social relations that bodies may have, and how each can impose limits on bodies. Bodies are constrained by their physical capacities (to overcome gravity, their need for nourishment and warmth, for example), and by psychological and emotional factors such as learnt patterns of behaviour, a need for human contact, feelings of loss or attachment and so forth. Social and cultural forces also play a large part in determining how bodies should act. Human cultures and civilizations have set out all kinds of rules and norms for human behaviour.

In this chapter, I shall look at control and management

of bodies. I will look first at how bodies have been classified, managed and organized in modern institutions, before
considering the effects of body organization, control and self-
discipline upon our behaviour, identities and even thoughts.
I will look also at how bodies continually resist the efforts to
manage and control them.

## Classified bodies

In most societies throughout history, bodies have been classified and categorized, into social groups, genders, ages or
ethnicities, for instance. This classification may be done by
the state, by professions and scientific disciplines such as biomedicine and social sciences, or by the citizens themselves.
Opportunities, legal and political rights, wealth and access
to power may depend upon a body's position in these classifications. Thus, for example, in eighteenth-century Britain,
women had no rights to vote, own property, or to enter most
professions, while racial differences have been the basis for
the oppression and even enslavement of bodies for thousands
of years.

Physical and other characteristics may be the basis for body
classification, most notably in terms of age, gender and ethnicity. 'Invisible' classifications such as caste position can be made
visible by applying marks to the face or body. In the absence
of such explicit, physical marks, bodies may be classified (and
self-classified) through subtle body markers of distinction,
including choice of clothes, cars and other possessions; diet;
leisure pursuits; or accents and vocabulary.

Many societies throughout history have been organized
around a class structure, which has been used to allocate
resources or to determine rights. Ancient Roman culture was
based around three classes: a patrician sect of ruling families;
the plebeians or common people; and finally, slaves. More
recent European societies differentiated between royal and
aristocratic classes, merchant classes and peasantry/workers,

with many gradations across this class spectrum. In some Asiatic cultures, castes replace classes: here bodies are differentiated by membership of social groups defined according to multiple criteria including occupation, class and ethnicity or tribal origin. Class structures normally favour the privileged class, allocating status, rights or resources unequally across the class divide. Class systems change and evolve over time, and the emergence of democracy, universal voting and other rights have tended to reduce the effects of class in many societies. Think for a moment about the influence that ideas of social class may still have on society, and whether this is based on wealth, social position or other factors.

Scientific disciplines such as sociology and epidemiology have been willing to adopt 'class' (or more accurately 'socioeconomic status' or SES) as a concept, based upon a range of social, economic and occupational criteria, and have used these classifications to explain social structures and patterns of achievement by individuals (Savage 2000: 3–6). For example, studies suggest that in the UK, class differences perpetuate inequalities in wealth, education, occupations and access to resources. Morbidity and mortality have been linked to socioeconomic class, with professionals at lower risk from almost all diseases and even accidents than those in non-professional occupations (Davey-Smith et al. 2002; Townsend and Davidson 1990). Social mobility across classes remains limited, and mechanisms have been suggested to explain how 'class origin' affects educational aspirations, choice of occupation, social influence and other life-chances, and how these repeat from generation to generation, perpetuating inequalities (Bourdieu and Passeron 1990).

We saw in the last chapter how 'sex' has been established as a two-way biological classification of male and female, while 'gender' described the psychological and social experiences of masculinity and femininity. Most cultures have used this binary classification of bodies to allocate roles, privileges, rights and duties differentially. Ever since Eve (having succumbed to bodily temptation in the shape of a forbidden apple) was cast as the mythic cause of Man's [sic] fall from grace, female bodies have often been considered as inferior physically, morally or intellectually, with differences in access to resources or rights following from these beliefs (Greer 1971).

In the West, political emancipation (the right to vote and participate in public life) and the rise of feminist movements has slowly led to narrowing in pay and employment rights and changes in public and private attitudes, while advances in contraception enhanced female sexual freedom, and laws provide women with rights to property and protect them against sexual or other violence in domestic settings. Despite these advances, fundamental differences in social attitudes to men and women remain, which can affect access to resources, norms of behaviour and expectations of bodies. While institutional sex discrimination is now illegal in most societies, sexism persists in terms of how men and women are valued, and how they are expected to behave and comport themselves. Women in politics, business and industry have sometimes hit a 'glass ceiling', an invisible barrier to their progression to the highest positions. In some cultures, women's opportunities to participate in daily life are tightly constrained by religious or cultural expectations concerning clothing, deportment and behaviour. Even in the West, different standards of behaviour may pertain for men and women. Can you think of examples from your own experience of this?

Ethnic characteristics of bodies have also been used to classify individuals into 'races', a concept given pseudo-scientific legitimacy during the Victorian period with the emergence of the discipline of anthropology. Racial classifications emerged alongside increasingly frequent contacts between nationalities, as markets became global in the middle ages, and Europeans expanded their empires into Africa, Asia and Australasia. Skin colour and body shape have been used in many cultures to classify racial types, and to allocate privileges, rights and resources between peoples (Connolly 1997: 66; Neal 2000).

Proscriptions on inter-racial interactions and miscegenation (sexual contacts or marriage between races) have followed from ethnic classifications, with slavery, the Nazi Holocaust directed at Jews and Gypsies, and racial apartheid as extreme outcomes of this kind of classification of bodies.

From time to time, claims have been made by biomedical scientists and psychologists to have identified underpinning differences between ethnic groups, in terms of intellect, physical prowess and so forth. These arguments fuel the ideologies of racist and far-right political groups such as the Ku Klux Klan in the US and neo-Nazi groups in Europe, and the thoughtless racism that can affect communities, often based in fear or economic stress. The latter may have a daily impact on the lives of people in terms of employment, opportunities or even physical safety.

## Coercion and discipline

In addition to these 'stratifications' of embodiment in terms of class, gender and ethnicity, bodies are also subject to intrusive control of behaviour. From birth onwards, human bodies are shaped to fit into cultural norms and expectations, from a gender identity as male or female through to the acquisition of language and training in the cultural rules of a particular society. The latter extends from rules of politeness and decorum such as 'table manners', modest behaviour or respect for elders or authority, through to more detailed culture-specific knowledge and understanding.

Historical and sociological studies of societies and cultures from prehistory to the present have exposed the systems of power and control that imposed order on their citizens' bodies, usually in order to maintain top-down control by a sovereign or ruling elite. In earlier times, and in some non-democratic societies today, this control was based upon extremes of coercive (forceful) power, exercised by those with wealth, authority or political or military influence. Harsh laws were used to protect these privileges and control those in lower orders, quashing any resistance to sovereign power by violence or judicial authority. As recently as two hundred years ago in the West, crimes against property such as burglary or theft (now punished by short spells of imprisonment or fines) carried a sentence of death or transportation to the colonies, while those challenging the authority of the ruling classes might expect horrific (to modern sensibilities) bodily punishments, involving mutilation, torture and death (Foucault 1979: 3). Coercive power was also manifested in the medieval judicial system, with torture widely used as an interrogation technique and as a weapon of state terror, instilling fear in those contemplating a challenge to social order (ibid.: 40). This kind of exercise of force upon bodies was also a feature of punishment in schools until quite recently, as we will see later in this chapter.

Such cruel physical punishments are far less common today, although torture from 'water-boarding' to mutilation is still in use during political interrogation in many countries. The historian and philosopher Foucault suggested that the change from extreme body punishment to more 'humane' systems, in which imprisonment is more widely used and torture outlawed, marks something other than the gradual civilization of law and order. He suggested that it also indicates a fundamental shift from a top-down coercive power, to a more 'democratic' exercise of *discipline* throughout the population, no longer by a ruling elite but on behalf of society as a whole. Coercive power remains, but is used less and less, because disciplinary technologies have proven more effective in sustaining general social order and reducing resistance than the reign of terror and barbarism they succeeded. The objective of disciplinary power was to create what Foucault called 'docile bodies' (ibid.: 136).

Crime and punishment are the most obvious areas where this change can be observed in the emergence of a modern society, but Foucault looked much more widely for evidence of this shift. In a lifetime's work devoted to exploring bodies and how these are subject to power and discipline, Foucault examined a range of institutions and professional perspectives on the body in modern society. Prisons, workplaces, schools and hospitals interested him, because he saw in them techniques developed to impose discipline over bodies. Part of this involved subjecting bodies to strict regimens, often governed by the clock and perhaps involving precise movements as on a factory production line or an army parade ground. Prisoners, soldiers, school students and patients all have fixed daily routines, developed to establish order and a sense of allegiance to the institution. Think about your own daily timetable (to fit into school, college or work) and how this governs your life.

A further aspect of disciplinary institutions was surveillance of their inmates, be they prisoners, patients, school students or the mentally ill. Foucault called this the 'gaze' of disciplinary power (Foucault 1976: 89). Today, technology such as closed circuit television (CCTV) means that bodies are under far greater surveillance than ever before, but in the past, buildings such as hospitals and prisons were often designed to enable easy observation of patients or prisoners. In the traditional 'Nightingale' ward, beds were ranged around the walls of a large room, with a 'nursing station' located centrally to allow a single nurse to observe beds throughout the ward. In addition to the watchful eye of the ward nurse over his/her patients, hospitals now apply many other technologies of observation, from clinical examination of patients through to monitoring devices and remote sensors to gather information about the bodies of their inmates, and use this information to create knowledge about bodies themselves.

Schools similarly observe, assess and document students throughout their education, offering remedial action if progress is deemed unsatisfactory. In the workplace, workers are subject to regular reviews and reports by managers to assess their performance and productivity. All these institutions document, analyse and record their subjects in great detail, framing these records within the professional model of its subjects (for instance, a medical record framed by biomedicine, or a set of a student's examination results framed within educational theory), to create what Foucault (2002: 145) called an *archive*.

Foucault has suggested that, as a result of the gaze and the archive, the modern body is a 'contested' entity in contemporary society. As we saw in chapters 1 and 2 of this book, medicine, theology, science, sociology, anthropology, psychology and other academic subjects with an interest in the body all have competed in the modern, post-Enlightenment period to describe, document, analyse and define the human body and its functions (Foucault 1970). These disciplines then claim to speak a truth about the body, perhaps to speak *the* truth about the medical body or the criminal body and so on. In the process, this knowledge of bodies becomes a 'body of knowledge': archives of evidence and theory that can be used to discipline our bodies into one form or another (Foucault 1979: 37–8).

To explore how bodies are managed in modern society, I shall now look at some of the arenas within which bodies are subject to disciplinary power.

## Working bodies

The routine of daily work, which may involve signing in and out to ensure that hours worked match wages or salary paid, is a modern invention. Most working bodies are subject to a discipline of attending work between specific hours, although for professionals there may be a flexibility to hours worked, based upon 'self-discipline' and a sense of duty. For many health care professionals, shift work is a fact of working life, with the rest of life fitted around the beginning and end of a shift. Large organizations such as health services or industries require a workforce that can be relied upon to staff the workplace, whether that is a clinic, a factory production line or an office.

The seeds for the discipline of working bodies are often

traced back to a military monarch, King Frederick the Great, who ruled Prussia (part of modern Germany) from 1740 to 1786. Frederick was fascinated by automata: mechanical figures whose clockwork insides enable them to perform repetitive actions. His desire was to mould his army so that it would perform as if they too had clockwork to govern their movements, rather than free will and muscles. Armies at that time were a rabble: shambolic, undisciplined and inefficient. Frederick introduced ranks and uniforms, regulations, standardized equipment, a command language, and army drill (Morgan 1997: 23–4). By these measures, he turned a collection of individual bodies into a disciplined and reliable fighting force which would obey orders and achieve military objectives. His innovations laid the groundwork for today's 'professional' armed services.

Frederick's idea of managed, regimented bodies found a new focus with the birth of the industrial revolution during the early nineteenth century. Patterns of work were revolutionized in this period, with factories recruiting millions of people who had previously worked in agriculture and 'cottage industries'. Making cloth is a good example of how work changed during this period. Before the rise of mills and factories, weaving took place on a small scale, on a loom in a workshop or upstairs rooms of domestic cottages. There was little need for workplace discipline: people sold what they made and got a price regardless of how long they had worked at a job. But once 50 or 100 looms were gathered into a water- or steam-powered factory, work had to change. There had to be bodies to work the looms so that expensive machinery would not lie idle. Workers could be paid for the length of hours worked, not for the numbers of goods finished. For the first time, work and time became linked together, with bodies now controlled by clocks rather than dawn and dusk. In a mill, disciplined bodies performed not military drills but repetitive actions for hours on end, working to the speed of the machinery, not the pace of their own choice. Factory whistles sounded the start and end of shifts and streets would throng with workers hurrying to and from the workplace gates.

The same was the case for other emerging industries like steel-making. A city like Sheffield grew within fifty years from a few small workshops powered by the city's rivers, to an inferno of forges and rolling mills fuelled by coal, turning out huge quantities of steel to meet demands from other new industries, transport, bridges and so on. With power available 24 hours a day, why not use the forges all day and all night, bringing in new shifts of workers to toil through the dark? The huge iron and steel rolling mills spawned spin-off industries everything from industrial tools, to garden implements, to cutlery and surgical instruments. Cities sprang up as millions of houses were built around factories to accommodate these immigrants from the country. Life centred on work, and bodies were subject to a degree of daily control in and out of the workplace.

Workplace control of bodies took another leap forward with the ideas of a second Frederick: Frederick Taylor, an American engineer who advocated five principles of work organization:

1. Shift responsibility for the organization of work from the worker to the manager. Workers implement, managers think
2. Use scientific methods to determine the most efficient way of doing a job, and specify exactly how the work must be done
3. Select the best person for the job
4. Train the worker to do the job efficiently
5. Monitor worker performance to ensure procedures are followed and appropriate results achieved. (Morgan 1997: 30)

Taylor broke down jobs into the smallest possible components, and used time and motion studies to fit them together into an efficient process aimed at producing a standard outcome. Under Taylor's regime, a worker now became responsible for a single step in a manufacturing process. Each worker focused on the specialized task; work was de-skilled with lower-paid workers trained in a single operation replacing craftspeople. To some extent this has also occurred in health care, with professionals (for instance, physiotherapists, midwives and dieticians) becoming more specialized in their work, and medical expertise divided into specialisms such as gerontology and paediatrics.

Taylorism was taken a step further by Henry Ford, the car manufacturer who innovated the production line. On a production line, work comes ceaselessly to the workers, who must work at the speed of the line, not *vice versa*. In the 1960s, General Motors raised the speed of its production line from 60 to 100 cars per hour, and workers had to increase the speed with which they completed their tasks to match the line (Morgan 1997: 31). Now the workers were fully controlled by the machines! Although fewer people now work on production lines, Taylor's and Ford's legacies persist. Call-centre staff follow prescribed scripts as they interact with customers; MacDonald's workers are trained to perform precisely defined tasks designed to supply an identical product in every outlet. In office environments, workers perform repetitive data processing tasks (from word-processing to financial management) according to prescribed job roles. Quality assurance measures and guidelines in health care similarly define how tasks should be performed by nurses and doctors, which drugs should be used or which procedures to be followed, with limited freedom to exercise independent judgement. Workers are kept under surveillance by managers, who monitor performance and check output quality and quantities. Think about your own experiences of work: how were you made the subject of this kind of observation or review?

In two hundred years, work has been transformed from an individualistic activity to a specialized, highly regulated and quality-controlled task designed to maximize efficiency. Workers' bodies are disciplined in a lifetime devoted to labour, governed by the clock and rendered docile by a regular wage packet. The traditional presentation to a retiring worker in the UK of a watch or clock seems ironic: all their life they have been controlled by time, finally they are free of its mastery of their daily routine. A worker such as Alice Martin, who worked all her life apart from short spells of child-rearing, may feel abandoned and aimless upon retirement, so pervasive has the routine of daily work been on her body.

At the same time, work has become the subject of academic theory, with work psychology, the sociology of work, economics and social policy all focusing on work and working lives. The modern state has made work a major focus, as the means of creating wealth in a capitalist society. National insurance numbers document every worker within a national jurisdiction, while employment and unemployment statistics are key numbers for policy-makers and economic planning. Working bodies are thus surveyed and archived, subjecting their bodies to management and organization locally and nationally, throughout their lives (Adkins and Lury 2000: 161).

## Learning bodies

In modern cultures, understanding of the rules and laws of a culture, sexual norms of behaviour and the moral duties of a citizen may be left to parents and other more informal networks. I described in chapter 2 how together these systems progressively socialize the child from infancy to adulthood to become a useful member of a society. Preparation for the body discipline of the workplace also begins early in life. Responsibility for transmitting culturally important knowledge enabling people to function in the world of work has been delegated to professional educators in schools, while advanced training for a specific role in the workforce may entail college or university study or vocational qualifications. The history, geography, religion and social organization of a society, the techniques for communication, literacy, basic numeracy and an understanding of science and technology fundamentals are all part of a Western school curriculum, considered necessary for effective citizenship and efficiency in the demanding workplaces of a complex modern culture (Gordon et al. 2000: 81).

Schools emerged both to instil knowledge and skills and also to subject children to a regime of bodily discipline and surveillance (Deacon 2006: 184). Disobedience, immorality and bad behaviour were met with corporal (bodily) punishments, ranging from smacks to flogging, although these techniques were generally abandoned as inhumane and ineffective in the twentieth century. More importantly, schools have progressively disciplined students through the management of time. Timetables and a set daily schedule of lessons establish routines and rhythms to the school day, term and year, with time set aside for intellectual and physical development each week. Indeed, a whole school career may be graduated and measured out from first to final grade. Time management is coupled to surveillance: children are periodically evaluated against their same-age peers through techniques such as IQ tests, while regular tests and examinations assess progression against curriculum benchmarks, generating sets of marks to categorize and order students by performance, subject by subject. Termly reports serve both to inform parents of educational performance and to summarize progress. Schools became 'total institutions', governing more and more of a child's day. Punctuality was expected of students (Deacon 2006: 182), with lateness a sin worthy of punishment, possibly by detention.

> Like other disciplinary institutions, the early modern school attempted to exercise control over and responsibility for nearly all of its inmates' time, a principle rendered concrete by subsequent concerted interventions in pre-, post- and home-schooling, vocational training, Sunday schools, extramural activities and managed recreation, and taken to its logical conclusion in today's concept of lifelong learning. (Deacon 2006: 182)

Schooling has become the focus for a new educational science, according to Deacon (2006), in which advances in teaching methodologies, techniques of micro-disciplinary training of the body (for example, hand-writing or gymnastic competencies), the management of sexuality, the involvement of parents, families and society itself in a child's progress, and the reappraisal of curricula and learning all have become systematized and subjects for scholarly research.

The student's body, however, remains the focus of this science of education, whose aim is the production of a citizen with the moral, cognitive and physical attributes required by society. In today's context, this means ensuring that education produces high school and college graduates who possess transferable personal skills that will enhance employability and meet employers' needs as well as intellectual knowledge. In the US, school counsellors help students acquire life skills and emotional maturity, while in the UK, the introduction of vocational qualifications and apprenticeships aims to bridge the gap between school and work (Machin and Vignoles 2005), to render discipline and control of the body between these phases of embodied life seamless and non-problematic. Educational policy is at the forefront of most governments' minds, and perceived crises in the quality of schooling lead to frequent new policies, re-organizations and revisions to examination processes. Learning bodies are thus the objects of both micro- and macro-level management and control (Gordon et al. 2000). Reflect for a moment upon your own schooling: how did this discipline shape your body mentally, socially and physically?

## Medical bodies

Biomedicine was the subject of two of Foucault's studies of embodiment and discipline. Early in his career, he looked at the history of madness and its treatment, from imprisonment or exile through to the emergence of 'asylums' and psychoanalysis (Foucault 1971). He did not regard moves away from incarceration and inhumane treatments in the past to more enlightened psychiatric care as necessarily progressive. 'Enlightened' care regimes still sustain a distinction between the irrational behaviour of those with mental health issues and the supposed rationality of the rest of mainstream society. Madness still remains the 'other' in this equation (Foucault 1971: 264).

Foucault subsequently turned his attention to general clinical medicine, to examine the biomedical approach to health and the body (Foucault 1976). The birth of the modern clinic in the eighteenth century, Foucault argued, enabled the observation, documentation and classification of individuals within a medical setting. This in turn made possible comparisons between patients or the effects of different therapies. Physical examinations of patients and the use of monitoring technology contributed to a clinical *'gaze'*, and provided the basis to document the biomedical body fully (Foucault 1976: 9), creating in the process the *archive* of medical knowledge that I described in chapter 1.

Foucault's approach has been taken up widely within the sociology of health and illness. Armstrong (1983) looked at the rise of many modern medical specialties, including general practice, paediatrics, psychiatry and care of the elderly, while Nettleton (1992) examined dentistry, Arney and Neill (1982) studied obstetrics and Prior (1987) explored pathology from this perspective. In all these medical disciplines, a clinical 'gaze' observes and classifies bodies and their diseases, creating knowledge and at the same time establishing a regime of medical control over them. Armstrong (1983: 6) describes how this gaze emerged during the eighteenth century. The body

> ... was recorded in separate case notes, it was accessible because at this time medicine began to use methods of physical examination, it was analysable because pathology became localizable to a discrete point within the body, ... it was

subjected to evaluation because patients were moved from the natural focus of the home to the neutral domain of the hospital.

Armstrong (ibid.) goes on to argue that in the twentieth century, the emergence of public health and health promotion, and the technique of the epidemiological survey, extended this gaze from the hospital clinic into the hidden corners of the community, so that health behaviour (diet, smoking, exercise and so forth) in the wider population of bodies also becomes a legitimate focus for medicine (Bunton 1992, Petersen 1997) and dentistry (Nettleton 1992: 50).

While a biomedical model focuses predominately upon the physiological and biochemical functioning of bodies, the past fifty years have also seen the emergence of a more sophisticated *biopsychosocial* model of health and illness (Engel 2008; Fisher 1991), incorporating insights from psychology and social sciences to link biology, environment and behaviour. Biopsychosocial approaches have colonized general practice and are reflected in the emergence of popular health media, alternative and complementary therapies and health consumer products (Ogden 1995; Fox et al. 2005a; Fox and Ward 2008a). A *psychoneuroimmunological* model (Levin and Solomon 1990) offered an even more integrative and holistic connection between body, mind and behaviour, offering the prospect of a clinical science that might predict and perhaps control health and illness behaviour. The 'new' public health (Ashton and Seymour 1988) also focused on enhancing health at a population level, by encouraging good health through promoting positive health behaviours and identifying risks (Petersen 1997: 195).

For Foucault, these elaborations of a biomedical body to encompass psychological and social elements are part of the extension of a clinical gaze beyond the confines of the hospital or general practice into every aspect of daily life (Nettleton 1997: 208). The outcome of Foucault's clinical gaze is a medicalized, biological body which is synonymous with Deleuze and Guattari's concept of the body-*with*-organs, which I discussed in chapters 4 and 5. The body-*with*-organs (which Deleuze and Guattari also called the *organism*, to recall its physical, organic character) is – as we have seen – an assemblage constructed by body relations to biological and medical knowledge (Deleuze and Guattari 1988: 158). Biomedicine has been hugely significant in modern society for creating this conception of a body made up of organs, cells, genes and other molecules, in which behaviours, sexualities and even predispositions are seen as having biomedical roots.

## Managing the embodied self

Foucault's analysis of bodies, how they are organized, disciplined and controlled in modern society, and the relationship between disciplinary power and systems of knowledge such as biomedicine or educational theory, has provided an important perspective on embodiment and culture (Turner 1992: 10). Techniques (or technologies) of discipline, such as the gaze and the archive, act 'locally' on individual bodies and their moment-to-moment actions. However, this view of modern bodies as always the subjects of power and discipline may be criticized as over-deterministic, leaving little room for bodies to act independently (Fox 1998: 424).

Whether or not this criticism is accurate, it is certainly ironic, because Foucault himself was fundamentally interested in body strategies of resistance to power (ibid.: 425). Readers can, perhaps, see the problem for themselves in the brief outlines of body management in work, education and medical care above. By focusing on systems of power and knowledge, Foucault's versions of bodies seem remarkably passive in the face of discipline. To this, Foucault would have retorted that power emerges only where there is already resistance. Discipline in schools, prisons or clinics merely demonstrates the need to control and manage unruly bodies (workers or students want to take it easy, patients may not be willing to accept a medical definition of their condition or sit passively in a hospital bed). Rarely indeed does discipline fully establish docility in bodies.

Foucault's analysis of disciplinary organizations may best be used alongside the perspective of an active, resisting, creative body emphasized in this book. These descriptions of the controlled body can be seen as the other side of the coin from the exploration of desire in the last chapter. This connection becomes clearer in Foucault's later studies of how power and knowledge create a sense of identity in its human targets. This is the angle I now want to explore more fully. In particular, I will examine how biomedical power has contributed to a 'health identity' as a patient, how this identity is resisted, and the emergence of rival health identities.

Foucault turned his attention in his later work to the management of human behaviour and the conduct of individuals. This, he considered, had been achieved not just by techniques such as observation and documentation, but also by encouraging self-aware, 'reflexive' human bodies. The techniques of discipline that he studied (such as those described earlier in workplaces, schools and hospitals) work in part by creating citizens who 'self-survey', managing and controlling their own conduct from moment to moment, within broad guidelines on how to comport themselves. Foucault (1986) called this 'the care of the self', and traced how self-examination for moral or other flaws began with ideas of 'penitence' (regret for sins committed) in early Christian culture. Following confession of sins, penitents might go on pilgrimages to holy sites, or even subject their bodies to uncomfortable or painful rituals, in order to display their repentance. This transformed into private confession of sin to a priest (in which the admission of sin is itself proof of repentance). Foucault saw a further transformation of confession in the modern trend towards self-disclosure that has established such phenomena as psychoanalysis, therapy and even populist TV shows in which individuals or couples disclose their private lives to a charismatic presenter and an audience of millions (Foucault 1986).

However, this technology of the confessional is also the basis for a contemporary incitement continually to reflect upon and regulate one's conduct as an 'ethical' subject – monitoring, testing and improving the self (Rose 1989: 241). Modern society is replete with such encouragements, from maintaining a happy demeanour in the face of hardships ('keep calm and carry on'), an appropriate level of fitness and physical well-being (Glassner 1989), a good 'work/life balance' and so on. These 'technologies of the self' provide ways for individuals to manage their bodies, souls, thoughts and conduct, and transform themselves into happy, pure, perfected individuals (Huijer 1999: 69). Foucault came to believe that the creation of a reflective, self-examining and self-managing self was the basis for the 'docile bodies' of a modern society, much more than the exercise of either disciplinary or coercive power. He called self-surveillance *'governmentality'* (Foucault 1986: 162), to reflect the control, management or governing of bodies and selves.

I suggested in chapter 3 that we need to understand humans, bodies and 'selves' not as entities in their own right, but as always in relationship with their physical and social environment. Identity, according to this perspective, is not an independent 'essence' of who we are, but actually an outcome of a body shaped by assemblages of relations with its environment. The experience of self, of the 'I', comes into being as a result of links to 'truths and power' (Huijer 1999: 65–6). Foucault's detailed histories of power, knowledge and the body (with their focus on body management and organization) demonstrate both the ways in which disciplinary forces mould identity, but also how bodies self-manage, evaluate and censor what they can do, what they *should* do. As an example, let us consider briefly the part identity plays in managing a body's health risks.

## A case study: risk and identity

Modern bodies live within a 'risk society' (Beck 1992, 1994), in which almost every aspect of life has become filled with perceived dangers: physical, psychological, and moral, from hazardous carbon emissions causing climate change to the hazards to adolescent sexuality of pornography. Individuals have to continually assess the risks (the likelihood) of these hazards befalling them. In health care, more and more risks associated with hazards of living are being uncovered. There are risks from diets too rich in trans-fats, from smoking and alcohol use, from UV radiation, the side-effects of pharmaceuticals and so on. For health care workers too there are risks: risks from hazards such as blood products or the stress of clinical work. Some of the risks from these hazards depend upon individual behaviour: whether we smoke, have unsafe sex, what we eat.

Health education emerged over the past 100 years, and aimed to change people's behaviour, making them aware of health risks and how to avoid them. Health education and promotion act upon the anxieties of individuals to create 'risky' and 'safe' identities (Gastaldo 1997: 129; Nettleton 1997: 213). Unlike public health, health education gives responsibility for health (and for avoiding health hazards) to individuals, whether in sickness or in health (Petersen 1997: 117). In contemporary health education, it is up to individuals to assess the evidence from health experts and take control of their lives by acting upon it (ibid.: 215). Individuals must monitor inputs such as food, sleep and alcohol intake, and outputs such as exercise, time management and body shape (Petersen 1997: 200). People must reflect on risks and take responsibility to minimize exposure to health hazards.

Rose (1999) has called this the 'responsibilization' of life, in which more and more aspects of behaviour are subject to self-reflection and self-management. Evaluating risk establishes a moral dimension to bodily behaviour, creating a hierarchy between those who choose safe ways to manage their bodies and those who do not. Individuals are encouraged to 'care for the self', and blame may be attached to those who fail or choose not to take responsibility for their own health (for instance, for over-weight as a consequence of poor diet, or cancer due to smoking). In this way, a self-surveying identity (based on relations to hazards) becomes a 'technology of health' in the wider population beyond the hospital gates. Health education works by achieving the self-management of bodies and selves, without the direct intervention of health professionals.

We may imagine Alice Martin, the older adult with chronic osteoarthritis that I have considered from time to time in this book, in this context. Growing older has become a phase of life in which individuals self-manage, limiting their own activities to sustain their bodies' reduced capacities. Alice will adopt the health promotion messages that health professionals pass on, or that she sees in the media, taking mineral and vitamin supplements, getting regular but gentle exercise and so forth. She will feel responsible for her body maintenance and for ageing without complaint. She may even enrol in an 'expert patient' programme, so that she can actively try to maintain her own health, rather than just depending on the expertise of professionals. Alice 'governs' her own body, minimizing risks and behaving responsibly, according to health education messages. This leads us neatly to consider health identities.

## Health identities and body resistance

If my or your identity gives us a sense of 'who we are', then health identities refer specifically to our sense of ourselves in health and illness contexts. Health identities are assemblages of the core biological and social relations of health and illness that we looked at in chapter 4, along with 'the clustering of relations around specific aspects of embodiment, such as sport and exercise, body modification, disability or growing old' (Fox and Ward 2008b: 1010). Sexuality and the life course may also become part of a health identity (see, for example, Castells 2004: 294; Turner and Coyle 2000). Heath identities shape 'what else a body can do'.

Health identities may be quite dominant aspects of our wider identity, especially if we suffer from chronic illness or disability. Western societies are increasingly fascinated by all aspects of health and health care, from the 'cyborg technologies' (see chapter 8) of body modification by pharmaceuticals (Monaghan 2000; Potts 2004) or cosmetic surgery (Negrin 2002) to genetic therapies (Le Breton 2004) and cloning (Petersen 2002). Identity may often emerge within the context of these kinds of health-related practices. Health identities are assemblages created from the range of biomedical, cultural and philosophical aspects of health and health care that are a feature of contemporary culture (Fox and Ward 2006: 475).

Once upon a time, not so long ago, there was one dominant health identity: the 'patient'. The sociologists Parsons and Fox (1952) conceived of a patient's identity (constituted in relationship with a doctor) as similar to that of a child in relation to a parent: passive and dependent. Szasz and Hollender (1956) identified three models of patienthood: 'active-passive', 'guidance-co-operation' and 'mutual negotiation' that patients may adopt in their interactions with professionals. But things were changing. Watts (1975: 496) argued (in an era when all patients were obviously male!) that patients were becoming 'consumers', who

> . . . play a prominent role in much of the recent health care legislation, and the new legal doctrine of 'informed consent' gives the patient himself [sic] a decisive role in determining what will or will not be done in his own case. This is clearly another and significant change in the role of the patient – and the consumer, whether he is a patient or not – in health care.

Tuckett et al. (1985) described doctor–patient encounters as 'meetings between experts', in which the expertise of the professional in biomedicine met the expertise on the experience of illness of a patient. And by 2000, health policy-makers envisaged a future in which 'expert' patients might manage their own illnesses and conditions in partnership with their health and social care providers (Department of Health 2001: 5). People with chronic conditions can now receive training as expert patients (Shaw and Baker 2004), including:

- recognizing, monitoring and responding to symptoms;
- managing acute episodes and emergencies;
- using medications;
- adopting appropriate aspects of lifestyle including healthy diet, exercise and relaxation, and not smoking;
- interacting appropriately with health care providers;
- seeking information and using community resources; and
- managing negative emotions and responses to illness. (Wilson 2001: 134)

This list encapsulates exactly the kind of self-management that I described earlier when talking about health promotion and managing risk.

Meanwhile, a consumer movement has also affected the landscape of patient/professional interactions. Many medical conditions now have an advocacy or support network offering advice and information to sufferers. Numerous websites, interactive forums and email lists allow people to share information and discuss their condition and its treatment (Mendelson 2003; Mitchell 2003). This consumerist approach to health and illness has been fuelled by the development of treatments for so-called 'lifestyle' conditions, including male pattern baldness, erectile dysfunction and weight loss. In the UK, 'e-clinics' use online consultations to assess people's suitability for medications such as sildenafil (*Viagra*) or the weight loss drug orlistat (*Xenical*), before selling these products directly to consumers (Fox and Ward 2006).

Health and body identities depend strongly upon the cultural settings that supply relations for their assemblages. In a study of older adults in Australia and Thailand, Fox (2005) found that the physical, philosophical, social and cultural relations (with their beliefs, their families, their life experiences, their gender and ethnicity, their care and their bodies) constructed ageing health identities that differed markedly. Identities incorporated the effect of deteriorating health on independence, and experiences of health and social care provided by families, communities and professionals. Thai elders, generally speaking, coped better with dependency and the need for care than the Australians, due mainly to differing cultural and religious norms and values concerning ageing in the two communities (see pages 170–2).

Body shape as a relation within health identities was the focus of two studies by Fox, Ward and O'Rourke (2005a, 2005b). The first focused on those losing weight with the assistance of a number of proprietary and prescription drugs. The second looked at an online community of people with eating disorders within the 'pro-anorexia' movement. These studies supplied an understanding of health identities as intimately involved with the reflexive constitution of embodiment. For both those trying to lose weight as part of a diet, and those seeking to sustain a low body weight for reasons of self-control and self-affirmation, the relations were not only toward food, but also to social norms and to institutional attributes such as the authority of the medical profession.

Weight-losers became 'expert patients', knowledgeable about their condition but with a strongly medicalized health identity (Fox et al. 2005a). The pro-ana activists, by contrast, drew their understanding of their bodies and selves from a mix of science and cultural references. However, they did not share the underpinning focus on 'recovery' from anorexia in biomedicine, psychology and feminist perspectives. Instead, they saw anorexia as a *sanctuary* from a disordered life (Fox et al. 2005b). These studies suggested a continuum of health identities, from 'expert patient' to 'resisting consumer'. In another paper, Fox and Ward (2006) studied men and women using sildenafil (Viagra) either as a treatment for erectile dysfunction or to heighten and prolong normal sexual capacities and arousal. Again, these people fell along the continuum, with validation either from medical perspectives or from societal expectations concerning 'normal' sexual function (see also Potts 2004).

Health identities may become associated with all kinds of body practices. Vegetarianism, for example, is often more than a dietary choice, amounting to an identity that is sustained for a long period. Some vegetarians choose not to eat meat principally on ethical grounds of animal cruelty, while others see health benefits from a meat-free diet. A third group reject meat because of the impact of meat production on the environment. Fox and Ward (2008c) found fundamentally different identities between these groups, and occasional antagonism, with ethical and environmental vegetarians considering health vegetarians to be 'selfish', uninterested in wider concerns with animal rights or environmentalism.

What these studies suggest is that there are a variety of identities associated with health, other than the traditional, dependent identity of the patient. Nor are health identities limited to a fixed choice. Every individual's health identity is subtly different, emerging from an assemblage that is personal to them, and constituted from the disparate and unique combination of relations that a body has with its environment. One young man known as 'Andrew' studied by Fox and Ward (2008b) had two assemblages that affected his health identity:

identity – body – fitness – body size – embarrassment – training

an assemblage that framed his views of body shape and physical fitness, and

illness – medicine – identity – food and consumption – stress – fear

that framed the psychological and physical impact of a chronic illness from which Andrew suffered. Both established the limits of what Andrew's body can do, capacities that are shaped by his reflective self-consciousness of who he is, and of his relationship to other bodies and things.

Despite this, there is a tendency for biomedicine to impose its own version of health identity on those who become its subjects. The 'patient' is a convenient model of health professional, docile, dependent, compliant and subordinate to medical expertise. Professional power has been relinquished grudgingly; even the notion of an 'expert' patient was too rich for some physicians, who preferred the term 'autonomous' (Coulter 2002) or 'resourceful' (Muir Gray and Rutter 2002).

Within the broader approach developed in this book, however, we must recall that while bodies and selves are shaped by experiences and environment, we also play a part in making ourselves. Bodies may be a focus for control and management but this is a consequence of the unruly creativity of bodily desires, as we saw in chapter 5. There is always the possibility for *resistance* to forces, whether physical, biological or social, and efforts to manage bodies reflect the reality that bodies are not docile, that they are always in flux, always capable of becoming 'other'. For human beings, assemblages of relations shape what a body can do, yet the same assemblages may also be the basis for resistance. A vegetarian identity may limit a body to a meat-free diet, but it also establishes the body in opposition to dominant dietary practice and a food culture focused around meat.

## Conclusion

In this chapter, I have looked at how the body is controlled and managed and, in the earlier part, I examined the role that modern institutions such as the workplace, school and hospital play in this discipline; creating 'docile' bodies that are governed by aspects of the culture within which they are located. However, we have also seen how bodies self-manage and how this affects what a body can do. Self-surveillance and reflection on how a body should conduct itself have become ingrained in contemporary culture. Identity, including health identity, emerges from the assemblages of relations bodies have with the world around them. Identity establishes continuity and stability to embodiment that contributes to the daily management and conduct of bodies, quite independent of the forces explored earlier in this chapter. Our bodies govern themselves.

From the perspective of the health professional, it is important to recognize that the body is a focus for control and discipline, specifically, and perhaps especially, in health contexts. Health care may contribute to this control, directly through the technologies of surveillance and the archive that we explored earlier, or indirectly by creating health identities such as 'patient' or 'consumer' that limit what a body may do. However, while care may be a constraining force on bodies in some circumstances, it may also be a force that supports resistance and enhancing body capabilities. It is to this paradoxical dual character of caring that I turn in the next chapter.

### Suggested further reading

Foucault, M. (1980) The eye of power. In Gordon, C. (ed.) *Power/ Knowledge*. Brighton: Harvester.

Fox, N. J. and Ward, K. J. (2006) Health identities: from expert patient to resisting consumer. *Health*, 10 (4), 461–79.

Jones, C. and Porter, R. (eds) (1998) *Reassessing Foucault: Power, Medicine and the Body*. London: Routledge.

# CHAPTER SEVEN

# Caring Bodies

Every human body will receive care from others during their existence and most bodies will also be providers of care at some point. Parents care for their children's bodies from birth to independence; these children may in turn care for the parents when old or infirm. During illnesses, our bodies may receive care from professional or informal (lay or non-professional) carers, and we may also perform caring tasks on a daily basis for our friends, family and lovers, from a massage to preparing a shared meal. We may provide informal care to our colleagues or others: for instance, I may have pastoral responsibility for my students in the university, and may support my co-workers through personal or professional troubles. Think for a moment about your own experiences of caring and what is included in this idea. What does it mean to care? And what is the significance of being a caregiver or a recipient of care?

The sociologist Carol Thomas (1993: 649) offers an interesting distinction between emotional 'caring *about* someone' and the more practical act of 'caring *for* someone'. She suggests that on one hand, caring is based in intimate and human relations that value giving, love and concern. On the other, it is a set of practices – and theories about those practices – which have been codified by the 'caring professions' as the basis for an occupation and, on occasions, for control and authority (Gardner 1992).

For health professionals, this can be a problem. The care work they provide can be based on 'caring about' another person and what happens to them, but it is always also a professional activity governed by knowledge and guidelines about how to 'care for' patients' or clients' bodies. Sometimes the latter can get in the way of the former, so that the supportive, giving part of care is lost beneath the instrumental demands of a busy working life (James 1989). At worst, caring for a body becomes merely a task to be performed as efficiently and effectively as possible. From time to time, examples of 'care' that is deeply uncaring (often affecting the most vulnerable bodies – of children or older people) catapult into the law courts and the media. Such horrific examples of careless care cast a shadow over the positive elements of care, and the investments by millions of carers (lay, voluntary and professional) who daily supplement their physical efforts with love and generosity of spirit.

In this chapter, I shall explore what it means to give or receive care. For health and social care professionals, this is of immediate relevance for their interactions with the bodies of patients and clients. I will differentiate between instrumental, professionalized 'care' which entails some aspects of the management, surveillance and even discipline of bodies explored in chapter 6, and generous, positive, engaged 'care' that empowers and enables, and which motivates many to enter the caring professions. I want to look at these two faces of care and how they contribute to the caring assemblage, and explore the effects of care on the bodies of those cared for, in a case study of older people and the care they receive.

## Two sides to the caring assemblage

Human care is an activity that always takes place within a context. Whether it is the care provided by a parent to a newborn baby, the care given by nursing staff in intensive care or to a dying person, or the care received by Alice Martin when she attends the arthritis clinic, or from her family and friends in her home, the act of caring is surrounded by a set of physical, psychological, emotional, social and economic circumstances. These contexts shape the care that is given, sometimes in obvious ways (for instance, in terms of how professional care is provided and paid for), sometimes less obviously (the emotional impact of caring upon children who care for family members, for example).

Care as an unselfish and loving giving of succour and support in response to others' suffering (care-as-gift) may be traced back to Christian notions of love and charity. This was reflected in the early establishment of hospitals (originally these were houses of hospitality, in which medical care was incidental), alms houses and other charitable institutions throughout the Christian world (Dolan 1985). Similar traditions of charitable care and hospitals can be found in medieval Islamic culture (Dols 1987).

In the modern period, care in the West has been generally professionalized, with carers such as nurses, physiotherapists, occupational therapists, health visitors, social workers and so forth educated, often to degree standards, in the range of biological and social subjects considered necessary for effective care. Professional bodies, regulatory authorities and evidence-based guidance establish standards of care applicable to different diseases or conditions needing care. Research provides insight into the delivery of care and how it may be improved. Policymakers evaluate how care should be delivered, how it should be financed, and what should be the balance between lay and professional care responsibilities in society.

The twentieth century has seen an expansion in the availability of care services, but also a crisis in delivery and funding. The care that Alice Martin receives depends largely on where she resides. In much of Europe, health care is funded either through state or private insurance schemes, while social care is dependent on a mix of state support and private funding. In the US, health and social care are more market-driven, with a mix of commercial and voluntary organizations delivering health care, with some sectors of the community consequently denied access to care services. In developing countries, large proportions of populations may depend entirely on family and friends for social care. Increasingly, the ability to pay may be the main factor in determining what care many receive, from child care for working parents, to respite care for those caring for family members with disabilities or chronic illness, through to access to the latest medicines.

In these various contexts, economics and politics affect the availability and delivery of care. When care is state-funded, downward pressures on care budgets have led to a de-professionalization of care, with lower grades of staff such as care assistants and home helps replacing graduate professionals such as nurses for the delivery of some elements of care (Baumann and Silverman 1998). These changes in employment also affect the class, gender and racial mix of carers. Alternatively, where costs of professional care are unaffordable by families, responsibility for care falls increasingly on family members. In particular, women must often balance work outside the home with care duties (Mackintosh 1979: 175). Family-based informal care that has traditionally provided a resource of cheap caring labour (everything from child-rearing to care of the elderly) has been sustained by governments alongside professional health and social care systems, as a means to limit costs. Pushing care of those unable to afford professional carers back into the home may further impoverish families where caring duties reduce opportunities to undertake paid work (Lloyd 1999: 62). With economic challenges to public sector spending and political pressure for smaller government, lay care is unlikely to reduce in importance in the immediate future.

With the emergence of professional care, social theorists have pointed to a second theme that has emerged in contemporary society: the de-humanizing aspects of 'uncaring care', in asylums, orphanages, special schools, old people's homes and so on. Goffman (1968) described the brutality of care in mental hospitals of his day, while negative labelling and 'stigmatization' (applying a negative value to patients with certain conditions such as obesity, HIV/AIDS or mental illness) imposed a second burden on those already vulnerable from illness or ageing (de Swaan 1990; Goffman 1990). Physical, mental and sexual abuse have all been documented in institutions established to care for the most vulnerable in society.

So care has a positive and a negative aspect. I have called these the *gift of care* (to recognize the generosity of a 'good Samaritan'), and the care *vigil* (acknowledging the watchful eye of the professional carer) (Fox 1995). They have in common that they act through and upon bodies. At the simplest level, care establishes a relation between two bodies, a carer and a recipient. For instance, a parent will care for a newborn infant, providing physical nourishment, warmth and protection, but also an emotional and psychological engagement that links the bodies of parent and child in a mutual relationship. Both bodies affect and are affected by the care that is given and received. There are other relations at work here: for example, there will be a relation to the home environment, to the doctors, nurses and midwives involved in the delivery, and to the other parent, whether involved or not in the child's care. The child may represent abstract ideas also: love, sharing, the family, the future, the investment in a pregnancy and future child-rearing and so forth, and the parent will have relations to these concepts. As ever, the relations are unique to the specific caring circumstances and the individuals involved.

Continuing with this example for a moment, these relations of caring contribute to the care assemblage that shapes the bodies of the parent and the child. For a newborn infant, the assemblage will still be very simple, based on relations to milk, the mother's breast, warmth and comfort. For the parent, the assemblage will be far more complex, encompassing the baby's physical body and what it stands for, and all the relations mentioned above that surround the care provided to the infant. It will no doubt incorporate some anxieties and fears, and relations to professional and lay knowledge about care of a new baby and child-rearing practice. As time passes, the assemblages alter, and for the child, the assemblage will grow more complex to incorporate physical, emotional, psychological and social relations to the body of the parent and to the wider context of the home, school and beyond. For the parent, the assemblage will modify, allowing more autonomy to the child as s/he matures and eventually becomes an adult.

This way of understanding of care can be applied to all the variety of caring, from informal care between friends, lovers and family, to the professional care offered and received in hospitals, nurseries, day-care centres, residential care, hospices, and other institutions. It may even be applied to abstracted 'caring-about', the care we invest towards people, animals or issues in general, where we do not even know personally or have direct links to the bodies concerned. In each case, caring relations establish assemblages on the bodies of carer and recipient. Indeed, the body of the other party in the caring interaction becomes part of the assemblage: caring attaches bodies to each other.

As we have seen in earlier chapters, assemblages shape 'what else a body can do': the limits of possibility (or territorialization) of embodiment. They also affect identity (the sense we have of who we are), and in the context of health and illness, the health identities of the body (see chapter 6). For recipients of care, the caring assemblage can be all-important in determining the ways in which children, older people, and those who are sick or vulnerable experience their lives. So too for the providers of care, the caring assemblage will territorialize the body, perhaps making the experience a chore or a delight, or just a job of work. Because the relations within a carer/cared-for interaction vary, so will the assemblages. Despite this, it is possible to identify some core relations that may influence the caring assemblage. In what follows, I will explore the ways in which the settings of care influence the kinds of relations bodies have within care episodes. In particular, I will look at the kinds of assemblages that occur in professional care situations, how these may affect the character of care, and how it is experienced.

# The development of professional care

Foucault's studies of disciplinary power in hospitals, prisons and asylums, which we looked at in the last chapter, remind us of the two separate (but related) meanings of the word 'discipline'. Foucault suggested that systems of knowledge both establish the basis for a professional or academic discipline such as medicine, nursing, economics or psychology, and impose control and discipline over its members' and clients' activities and practice. Medicine, law and religion were early examples of 'disciplines' (or 'professions') and, in each, not only is there a 'body of knowledge' that establishes the authority of doctors, lawyers and priests to practise on their clients, but also a 'knowledge of bodies' that sets out guidance on how the bodies of professionals and their clients should behave and be organized.

The attribution of the label 'profession' to a job of work brings with it status, authority, autonomy and enhanced salaries (Freidson 1983). During the twentieth century, caring occupations such as nursing, midwifery, clinical psychology and paramedical groups have been keen to follow medicine and professionalize. Caring occupations were often staffed by women, and care was for a long time considered to be fundamentally female in character (Latimer 2000: 121). Care was seen as body-work (Twigg 2000), meaning 'dirty' work concerning the physical body and its functions. In a gendered and sexist society, this has meant both that there has been a gender bias in the proportion of males and females providing care, and that caring occupations have often been low in status (Freund et al. 2003: 277). Even in 2000 a nurse's salary in the US is about one quarter that of a physician (ibid.: 280). For caring occupations, professionalization often meant recognition of their work as independent of, or different in character from medicine, although the latter discipline has been slow to relinquish control over its patients to other disciplinary groups (ibid.: 277).

A fundamental prerequisite for professionalization is to establish a distinctive area of expertise, one not already claimed by another professional grouping. The nineteenth-century nurse Florence Nightingale's legendary mix of compassion and meticulous organization of nursing care established precisely this arena, and made her the first professional carer, although it has taken 150 years for nursing to be accepted as a profession. Nightingale set about turning a chaotic, poorly paid and menial occupation (nurses were regarded as equivalent to domestic servants) into a respected vocation in which values of service and responsibility were expected and delivered (Parker 1999: 41). Nursing was codified and new standards established for dress, hygiene, behaviour and duties. She also established the 'Nightingale ward', a design in which beds ranged around the walls of a light, airy room could all be observed by a vigilant nurse positioned at a central nursing station.

Gardner has suggested that professionalism endows caring with an authority it did not previously possess (1992: 251), and it was explicitly this *caring* dimension that helped to establish the independent practice area of nursing. This means that the history of care work from Florence Nightingale to the present day is two-fold. On one hand there is the history of care activity itself (the development of hygienic wound-dressing or the routines of daily nursing care, for example), but there is also a parallel story to be uncovered of control and the establishment of a body of knowledge about 'care' and care's clients. In other words: a history of the professionalization of body-care.

In the last chapter we saw how technologies of surveillance (the 'gaze') and documentation of patients, school students, workers or criminals (the 'archive') supplied the raw materials for the professions of biomedicine, education, work psychology and so forth. Technical skills and practical experience are not in themselves sufficient to create the crucial body of knowledge an occupation needs to achieve professional status. According to Shrock (1982), occupations aspiring to professional status

> emphasize relevant and appropriate research activities, attempt to construct a theoretical basis for their activities, (and) identify concepts, principles and theories. (1982: 104)

Nursing offers a good example of the development of a professional care discipline over the past fifty years. During this period, nurse education has become more academic, often relocated to universities from hospitals (Chua and Clegg 1990: 161).

You can find evidence for nursing's aspiration to professional status in textbooks of nursing philosophy. Take, for example, Gray and Pratt's (1991) *Towards a Discipline of Nursing*. This was published to coincide with the move of Australian pre-registration nurse education from a hospital-based to an academic setting (a move that has also occurred in North America and much of Europe). In their introduction, Gray and Pratt outlined their programme for the fabrication of a knowledge base for the discipline: it must adopt science as its framework, to achieve the goals of research, education and development of skills as scientific investigators as well as clinical expertise (1991: 4–8). Other contributors to the book discussed the contribution of philosophical theory to the making of the discipline (Sims 1991: 51ff.), a distinctive model of health (Anderson 1991: 109), and a conceptualization of nursing that focuses on meeting patients' needs and patient-centred outcomes (Cameron-Traub 1991: 37).

These contributions seek to define nursing as distinct from medicine. A patient-centred approach offers a contrast with medico-centric (doctor-centred) practices, and is also a means to gather unique data on patients' bodies further to develop nursing theory. Promoting this perspective, Thomas and Dolan argued that the nurse, 'where appropriate, must be able to follow the client and be sufficiently skilled and adaptable to care in any environment, be it the ward, day case unit or community' (1993: 125). Later they suggested that this would mean that nurses will play a more pro-active role in the maintenance of health and in providing primary, secondary and tertiary health education. Nurses of the 21st century will be actively involved in directing change and be adaptable to a changing world without fear of that change. (ibid.: 129)

Educational qualifications also mark out the professionalism of nursing care. Strumpf and Stevenson (1992: 422) considered that an advanced nurse specialist in gerontology would hold, 'at a minimum, a master's degree in gerontologic nursing', and would, among other things, develop, offer and evaluate services; work with professionals and clients to explore and resolve ethical problems; provide professional leadership and education to other professionals, and collaborate, use and disseminate research.

None of this is intended, of course, to discourage nursing or other care professionals from seeking to establish a firm, evidence-based grounding for their discipline, nor to seek the benefits for themselves and their clients of professional status. There are good and principled reasons for generating care theory, to standardize care and prevent abuse and poor performance. But is there a downside to the technologies of surveillance and archiving that a research-led profession needs? Think back to chapter 6, where I discussed the 'medical gaze': the observation of patients by biomedicine. Does the professionalization of care contribute to a caring assemblage that manages and controls bodies receiving care?

Professionals relate to their clients differently from carers in a family or other lay setting. There is a gap between the caring professional and the people whom they care for, a divide that may make engagement and empathy harder to achieve in the caring relationship. Even being labelled as a client or a patient (Hugman 1991: 113ff.) creates a health identity that can limit what a body can do. Twigg (2000: 390) notes that ironically as nursing has professionalized, staff 'move away from the basic bodywork of bedpans and sponge baths towards high-tech, skilled interventions; progressing from dirty work on bodies to clean work on machines'. Inglesby (1992) summarized, rather tragically I feel, the kinds of relations a professional nurse might have.

> When a candidate at interview is asked why she [sic] chose nursing the correct answer is no longer 'I want to help people'. If that is what she actually feels it would be more prudent to talk about social obligations, nursing being a profession which involved relating to others, career mobility, academic and emotional gratification . . . The value upon care remains high, but care is no longer 'tender' and 'loving', it is a specifiable commodity . . . A nurse no longer has a vocation; she has a profession. She is no longer dedicated; she is professional. She is no longer moral; she is accountable. (Inglesby 1992: 54)

In a world of professionalized care, caring and cared-for bodies have relations to the professional, career and work patterns of carers, and to theory and evidence-based guidance that govern how care is to be performed. The assemblages that derive from these relations shape the bodies of carers and clients. That does not mean that professional care has to be devoid of qualities of empathy, generosity and engagement, although it may make it harder for these to shine through. Some writers have argued that there is within care the potential for relations that may counter the vigilant, evidence-based relations of professional caring, to open up possibilities for the bodies of care recipients.

## A gentler professionalism? The gift of care

Bodies in need of care are often forced into a position of dependency, in which the indignities of a loss of independence can be almost as debilitating as the illness or condition that requires them to be cared for. Yet these circumstances are precisely when a body needs support to break free from the illness and identity assemblages that are constraining (territorializing) what it can do. Professional care cannot always provide an individualized response to bodily needs: a 'tailored' care package based on theory and evidence-based guidelines may not be sufficient for a de-territorializing line of flight.

The idea of care as a gift stands in opposition to a professionalized care based on theory and guidelines derived from theory. Our English word 'care' derives from the Latin *caritas*, which means loving, gracious and, of course, charity, from which follows the sense of giving altruistically, without expectation of any reward or reciprocity. Early charitable foundations were based on this view of care as a gift given without any return, a notion that has its roots in Christian kindness and love. Gift relationships are altruistic (Cixous 1986), and have characteristics such as generosity, trust, confidence, love, benevolence, commitment, delight, patience, esteem, admiration and curiosity (Fox 1993: 92).

Many of these relations stand in contrast with what we expect of professional carers and may even be seen as *unprofessional* and inappropriate. Professionals do not simply care out of the goodness of their hearts, they are salaried, and perform their duties at least in part in order to earn their keep, develop a career and gain self-fulfilment (all of which, in turn, define what it means to be a professional). Where carers do not have a bond with those for whom they are paid to care, there may be a lack of emotional relations, or these relations may be repressed. De Swaan's (1990) study of a cancer ward suggests the difficulties of professional caring. Here the anger and fear of patients may be distressingly manifested, while the anxieties of staff caring for people who are dying are displaced or translated into medical terms. Patients' bodies are cared for, while their emotions go untended; staff avoid discussing their own upset with colleagues. Doctors and nurses learn not to become attached to seriously ill and dying people: the investment of care, affection and generosity by a member of staff in a patient goes 'unrewarded' when the next day the patient is dead (de Swaan 1990: 42–7).

However, de Swaan suggests that professionalism can

supply a *gift*, a moment of engagement that can de-territorialize the patient's embodiment:

> To patients it means much when doctors and nurses know
> how to handle their wounds competently and without fear.
> The nurse patiently washing a dilapidated patient, changing
> his clothes, is also the only one who dares touch him with-
> out disgust or fear, who quietly and competently handles the
> body which so torments and frightens the patient . . . (who)
> knows how to deal skilfully with the wounds and lumps, in
> doing so liberating the patients for the moment from their
> isolation. (ibid.: 48)

The *gift* of care is constituted in open-endedness, rather than
theory and evidence-based practice. It does not say what something is or is not; it allows, for a moment at least, a thing to
become multiple, to be both something and another thing and
another. Professional carers have the potential to provide a *gift*
that can provide its recipient with a resource with which to
challenge her/his situation. For example, Bunting describes
the care provided within a family working with a child with
special health needs:

> As the family members work with the child and with one
> another, each moves beyond the self and the present reality to
> the possibles that unfold . . . The family's health is the move-
> ment toward and the expression of these possibles, as they
> are chosen and lived. (Bunting 1993: 14)

In most professional care settings, negative and positive
aspects of care may be present to greater or lesser extents,
although there is always the potential for the positive, enabling
and empowering elements to become (intentionally or unintentionally) impersonal and controlling. To give an example:
in a therapeutic setting, a person undergoing treatment may
well invest trust and confidence in a therapist, who in turn
offers support and encouragement to the patient to take control of her/his situation, and break free of the constraints of
suffering and dependency. But if this support becomes codified through guidelines, professional standards or routine,

as may easily happen in institutional caring, then what was an empowering relationship becomes disempowerment, as a patient's body is managed and de-humanized.

This can also work in reverse. A carer may break from routine when working with a patient or client, perhaps simply by sharing a moment of laughter or empathy, turning professional care into a *gift*, if only for a short time. A moment of shared humanity (or recognition that we all have fragile bodies) can be enough to enable a line of flight that allows a patient to break from dependency. In part, it is this issue of how to resist the *vigil* of professional care that makes the exploration of caring bodies of relevance to all those involved in care: both as providers and recipients.

Caring contributes very significantly to the assemblages that shape the experience of health, illness and ageing. Both in institutional and lay settings, the body of the care recipient is the site of a struggle between the body's motivated, experimenting desire, and the assemblages that accrete from the relations it establishes and the forces that affect it. Professional carers may find themselves torn between the opportunities to support bodies to achieve creative lines of flight, and the demands of a job that all too easily turns bodies into objects to be observed, documented, categorized, evaluated and subjected to standardized 'care plans' (James 1989). We can see the effects on cared-for bodies when we look at older adults' experiences of care. On this occasion, rather than using our fictional case study of Alice Martin, we can explore some real data on care of older adults.

## Older adults and the experience of care

I introduced my research on older adults (Fox 2005) briefly in chapter 4. This research was based on fieldwork with older adults living in family homes or residential care homes in Australia and Thailand. I wanted to understand more about how the *vigil* and the *gift* of care worked, and how care was experienced by its recipients. Most Thai people are cared for in old age by their adult children, although a small proportion lives in state-run residential accommodation, usually because they have no family carers. In Australia, older adults either live independently in the community (with support from family and care professionals) or in care homes. Cultural expectations are very different: Thais draw on their Buddhist world-view, accepting ageing and loss of independence as a phase in the cycle of existence; while the Australians regarded ageing more negatively and try to retain their independence as long as possible.

For the Thai respondents, care provided by their families was expected and appreciated. Mrs G accepted the care she received, but retained her sense of independence.

> *Thai Mrs G:* I'm not dependent on my children, because I help myself with the things that I can do. My children give me food and take care of me, but I help myself first. I can walk, I can do anything.

Familial care was part of a system of duties within Thai culture that structured the life course. For Mr H, being cared for by his grown children was simply the way things were supposed to be.

> *Thai Mr H:* I don't feel strange, this is the way of life – we look after them when they are children, and now I am old they have to look after me. This is our lifestyle, it's their duty . . . even after my daughter got married she lives not far from here, they quite often ask about my eating, or my health . . . I am sure my son will stay with me, because when he gets married, he will bring his wife to stay with him.

However, familial care was not always so easy in practice. For one Thai man, living in his son's home and being financially dependent was marked by a very material problem: the struggle to get enough to eat.

> *Thai Mr P:* I would prefer to live on my own, or if I could be just with my son it would be OK, but it's my daughter in law,

if I buy something to eat then everybody eats my food! Old
people should be with their family, but my son has so many
people in the house. My son pays all the expenses and takes
care of me. Yesterday he took me to the hospital because I had
asthma. But I am lonely and do not get enough to eat. Every
day I watch the TV and read the newspaper.

For the Australians, realizing they must accept care weighed
more heavily, as it challenged norms of autonomy and
independence.

*Australian Mrs C:* You feel as if everything's taken from
you. That's what it seems like and it's very hard to accept.
But anyhow I've got used to it now. You've lost your independence. You've lost things. And you've got to rely on these
people. And that's all about it. You've got to just settle down
and get used to it, and that's it.

Like any institution, residential homes have systems and rules,
some designed for the safety of clients, others to smooth the
running of the home. Mrs Y felt pressurized by these rules and
self-disciplined her behaviour to fit in.

*Australian Mrs Y:* I've got some steps in that cupboard that I
can put up and stand on them but there's always the chance
that you could fall. They'd be very cross with me if they came
in and found me on the floor. You just have to be careful,
but you don't have to watch television if you don't want to.
And I don't. I think people think I'm a bit peculiar. Probably
I am.

Mr M also felt under pressure to make life easy for the staff,
not only to avoid being troublesome, but also to avoid reprisals.

*Australian Mr M:* The younger staff probably think: 'Oh,
come on. Let's get going.' You've only got a certain amount of
time that they have to do things. And if this old bloke's holding them up, well, they get a bit agitated. They've got a routine
to do every day, you see, and if they can't get on with their
routine, well . . . Some girls are very good, very caring, some
others it's just a day's work to them. Each person has got a
care list but in a lot of cases the girls don't even read it. They

don't know what they're supposed to do. But if you upset the girls, they can make it awkward for you.

In both Thailand and Australia, respondents described what made their care a positive experience. For the Australians, it was centred on the personalities of the carers themselves.

> *Australian Mrs A:* The people are special. They're always bright and cheerful and willing to help as much as they can. And the people like down in reception, people in charge of sections and that, they are all special sort of people. You have to be if you're looking after old people in all sorts of conditions.

For one of the few Thai interviewees living in a care home, the routines and dependency seemed reassuring. Mrs L took pleasure from being cared for by committed and loving staff.

> *Thai Mrs L:* In my mind I am still a school child because here we have everything, we have many activities. In the morning I come to the front of this home, and sing the national song, and at eight o'clock I go to the cafeteria here and at nine p.m. I go to bed . . . I feel good because the caregiver takes care of me, and a lot of people come to visit us and take care, and make activities for us. I used to think that people in these homes were people the family doesn't want. But now I don't think that, because a lot of people outside come to visit me, and make activities to entertain me.

Australian respondents offered perspectives on the qualities of a good carer, with a range of comments that reflect the notion of the *gift* of care.

> *Australian Mr O:* I think it's the old cliché 'Do unto others as you would have done unto you'. I can't go further than that. It's simply that.

> *Australian Mrs S:* I could care for you and say 'Come on and do this', rather than gently putting my arm around you and saying 'Just come on and we'll do so and so'. . . . I see it like comfort and it also gives you confidence and security. It certainly makes you feel a lot better than somebody breezing in and saying 'Now listen here. Just come on and we'll do this'.

These extracts support the dualistic character of care which has been developed in this chapter. On one hand, care can be disempowering because of a loss of independence, and the constraints of relying upon others, whether in a family setting or an institution. For some of the Australians, the codification and organization of professional care not only limited what they could do, but also imposed a health identity in which they self-managed their behaviour to avoid real or imagined sanctions from staff.

On the other hand, being cared for can be fulfilling and liberating. The epithets of generosity, patience and love were ascribed both to the care and the carers, and this was the case both for those living in family settings and in institutions. For many, it seemed that a positive outlook overcame any possible limitations deriving from a need for care. Again, for these individuals, their sense-of-self was open to new possibilities, and they benefited from the positive support from their carers to achieve as many of those possibilities as they could.

This case study offers support to the view that care can be both a constraint and a liberation, and that professional care may be both of these things: care-as-gift is not limited to informal care (indeed, care by family members can be deeply constraining on both parties, and resentment, anger and even physical abuse may occur in such circumstances). However much a regime of care aims to be supportive and empowering to some it will be constraining and oppressive, while others will find means for a line of flight even when ill-health or the constraints of an institution appear to limit what a body can do. It is also clear from the data that carers can contribute significantly to de-territorialization; they can supply *care-as-gift* in a smile or a kind word, or a gesture of support. Carers can be important allies, even when they are overwhelmed by the demands of their work and the routinization and institutionalization of professional care. As current or future health professionals, you will face the challenge of bringing together the two aspects of care. How can you keep this balance and make sure the care you provide is a liberation, not a limitation on those for whom you care?

## Care and the dying body

For health and social care professionals, sometimes the care they provide will be to bodies in the closing stages of life. This may be the case not only in institutions such as hospices devoted to the care of dying bodies, but in any health or social care setting. Whether expected or unexpected, progressing slowly or rapidly, death marks a change to a body that affects its environment before, during and after life has departed.

Throughout this book we have seen how the body is both natural and social. We have applied an approach which recognizes the body as dynamically constituted in confluence with the relations it has, be these biological, psychological or cultural. Assemblages of relations interact with the creative, motivated desires of the body to shape what (else) it can do. Although at the moment of death the body loses the creative desires that had carried it forward through its life, body assemblages do not dissipate at the moment of death. A body can have relations even after death, and can continue to affect the world around it, most obviously having effects upon those people who were close and are touched by the loss (Tomasini 2009: 258–61), but also witness the outpourings of grief after the death of a beloved public figure. For carers, be they family or professionals, the processes of dying and death are tied up with the dynamic character of embodiment, and with the dual character of bodies as natural and cultural. The perspectives on care developed in this chapter; the *vigil* of managed care and the *gift* of care that can carry a body out of its constraints and into a line of flight are relevant and critical for the care of dying as well as 'living' (or not-yet-dying) bodies.

Western societies have sometimes been described as 'death-denying', and scientific medicine has contributed to this, seeking more and more heroic interventions to defer death

(Nuland 1994: 61). Death, for medicine, can seem a failure (Seale 1998: 103), but for caring professionals, this perspective can be unproductive and potentially harmful for the last days of a person who is dying in an institution. Despite the importance of carers in the worlds of dying bodies, carers may be unwilling to talk to their patients about death. Strickland and DeSpelder (2003: 19) described four ways carers try to avoid responding when patients attempt to initiate discussions about dying or death: offering reassurance ('you're doing fine'), denial ('you've got nothing to worry about'), changing the subject ('let's talk about something more cheerful'), and fatalism ('we all have to die sometime').

Carers' discomfort with death, and their efforts to avoid engagement with the dying process, can have some strange consequences. In a classic study of hospital death, Sudnow (1967) described the 'premature social death' that befell dying people prior to their biological demise. Those around a dying person, including carers, would begin to treat the person as if s/he had already passed away, having already outlived their normal social rights to be acknowledged as a living human. Seale (1998) summarizes some of these findings:

> Staff spoke openly about the likelihood of death, bodies and autopsies in the hearing of immobile patients who were unable to communicate their understanding; a nurse closed the eyes of a person on the point of death, explaining that this can be harder to achieve after death has occurred; 'do not resuscitate' orders were posted on the basis of the perceived social value of the patient. (Seale 1998: 102)

The de-humanizing regimes of large medical institutions, an emphasis on the living over the dead in professional medicine, and a lack of training or support for professionals to cope with their own feelings about death all contributed to making death in hospital an impersonal and lonely experience. Since Sudnow's study, much effort has since been devoted to improving the care given to dying bodies, with training to health and social care professionals in how to interact and communicate with dying patients (Rushton et al. 2009). The rise of the hospice movement has also contributed to more enlightened care of those approaching death, addressing

> the social, spiritual, physical and emotional elements of care . . . which are usually obscured in medical settings, and require management and attention in the same way that physical symptoms do. (James 1989: 20)

James (1989) described the emotional labour that carers undertake in hospices, working closely with dying people and incorporating an emotional engagement with them, as part of a holistic approach to care that does not deny death, or the emotions it engenders both in the dying person and their carers. As Strickland and DeSpelder (2003: 19) suggest, a carer

> who steps into the room, sits by the patient's bedside, and demonstrates a willingness to listen, is likely to be more successful in providing solace and aid than the one who breezes in, remains standing, and quips, 'how're we today? did we sleep well?'

These approaches recognize the relational quality of embodiment, and that dying bodies are linked by a mesh of relations to their environment, including their carers. A dying person becomes part of a carer's body assemblage in the same way that carers are part of the dying person's assemblage. Carers are not immune from feelings of sadness, anger, guilt, fear and so forth. The carer who listens in a spirit of generosity to the dying person may also gain solace from the encounter, rather than avoiding or denying realities of mortality.

The messages concerning gifts of care discussed earlier are as relevant, if not more so, in caring for dying bodies. A moment of engagement by a professional carer with a dying person, for the latter perhaps their last moment, can be a line of flight for both. But as I suggested earlier, death does not mark the end of embodiment, nor do a dead body's assemblages evaporate at the moment of death. Body assemblages may continue to influence the body-without-organs of a dead person, most notably in the funeral rites and memorials that commemorate them and may determine what becomes of physical remains (Tomasini 2009: 260). At the same time, dead bodies will also be relations for other living bodies into the future, affecting the living in many ways as the dead are remembered or influence behaviour of those left behind. For those experiencing the death of a body close to them, be it a family member, a friend or a patient or client, that body will continue to affect them even after the physical presence is departed.

Health and social care professionals must learn to accommodate the dead in their own assemblages, and recognize the influence of the dead on who they are, and how they understand their own lives, bodies and mortality. Death is a subject many of us try to avoid even thinking about, but as you read these words, reflect for a moment on your own feelings about death, and how you might develop these so you can be more supportive to dying people and to those left behind by a death.

## Conclusion: What can a caring body do?

This chapter is of relevance for every current or future health or social care professional. I have shown how care can be either a limit on the body that closes down possibilities or provide the 'nudge' that allows a body constrained by illness or other circumstance to break free. Although all care has this capacity to be either a limit or a line of flight, the emergence of professional caring has thrown this duality into sharper focus. Professionals have the capacities to significantly affect positively or negatively the experiences and life-chances of those for whom they care.

The vigil and the gift of care contribute to alternative caring assemblages. These assemblages shape what the bodies of care recipients can do, and their effects may be incremental, feeding back positively to increase respectively dependency or independence. For those who, like Alice Martin, are recipients of care, the vigilant scrutiny of their lives, the imposition of regulatory frameworks, and the social relations between provider and recipient of material support construct a network of dependency that can easily lead to further dependency (Biggs 1997: 559). On the other hand, a gift of care can challenge boundaries and limits – be they physical, psychological or emotional (Gibson 2000: 778). We saw the importance of such gift relations in ameliorating dependency in the case study of older adults in this chapter. This too can create a positive feedback loop, enhancing independence and a 'line of flight' from dependency.

Caring bodies can use the relations with those for whom they care to achieve this end. Sometimes these relations are fully intentional, for instance in the case of a psychotherapist who uses a cognitive or behavioural technique to de-territorialize the client's body and what it can do. Other times, they are unintended, like the smile or the moment of sharing by a carer that some respondents in the case study said was so important to them. We all of us may have been agents in this way, and not even know we have given a gift. However, the evidence is that caring bodies can also affect the recipients of care negatively, particularly where their behaviours or interactions tend to create assemblages around identity that are fixed, determined or narrowly defined. All of us, carers or not, do this all the time with the people we meet or otherwise affect. It is quite a responsibility.

One final thought. Caring bodies are themselves shaped by assemblages that set the limits on what their own bodies can do. Caring can be hard, especially where investments of time, energy and 'emotion management' in recipients of care are part of the job. Some carers manage the physical, psychological and emotional territorializations of their work by stepping back into detached professionalism, or by using props such as drink or drugs to forget for a while. Others develop networks of support that can help to share the burden. Even carers need to be cared for; and support and mentoring can provide the gift that allows a line of flight for the carer too.

### Suggested further reading

Latimer, J. (2000) *The Conduct of Care*. Oxford: Blackwell Science.
Parse, R. R. (1992) Human becoming: Parse's theory of nursing. *Nursing Science Quarterly*, 5 (1), 35–42.
Twigg, J. (2000) Carework as a form of bodywork. *Ageing and Society*, 20 (4), 389–411.

CHAPTER EIGHT

# The Body and Technology

The body depicted in previous chapters of this book may have seemed to stand alone, naked; growing up and growing old; desiring; controlled; cared-for. However, modern bodies surround themselves with the fruits of human ingenuity and labour: clothed, housed, kitted out with comforts and gadgets, fed with the products of cookery or the local take-away. Bodies are rarely, possibly never, without technological products. In work, leisure, creativity and sport, bodies continually push their limits, but usually with the benefit of technology: the tools of the trade; the wizardry of digital electronics; musical instruments or artists' materials; a ball, a bat or a riding crop. We literally surround our bodies with technology.

Technology is *the knowledge and use of tools and techniques to enable or enhance bodily action.* Human bodies have applied technology for thousands of years to increase their capacities and mastery of the environment, to overcome the limits that nature imposes. It is hard work digging over a field by hand: so invent a plough and harness a horse's power to do the job in a fraction of the time; invent a tractor and apply 100 horse-power to the task. Modern bodies surround themselves with technology that makes life easier; that creates more wealth for the same effort; that improves our health, happiness and longevity.

As appropriate for a book aimed at health and social care professionals, in this chapter I will explore the technology found in health care institutions: the tools, techniques and equipment used to detect, diagnose and treat disease, from medical devices and equipment such as inhalers, monitors and body scanners, surgical techniques and instruments, to pharmaceuticals and alternative/complementary treatments. But I will focus most specifically upon those *body technologies* that integrate closely upon or even *within* bodies, to assist, support and even enhance body functions and processes, creating 'cyborg bodies' that transcend biological limitations and might herald a new 'trans-human' body (Fuller 2011).

So in this chapter I shall explore the part technology and the consumption of technology plays in de-territorializing bodies from their physical limitations, and consider the consequences for embodiment of a close association with technology. Body technologies offer the promise of freeing a body from biology, overcoming impairment and perhaps enabling different embodiments, unconstrained by the physical properties of cells, organs and anatomy, or the 'normal' functions of the body. But can the emergence of intimate technologies of the body have a downside too? The integration of technology upon and within the body may actually apply new limits to the body, as defined by the designers and engineers behind the technology. Could technology territorialize the body, rather than enhancing its capacities? How may 'cyborg bodies' alter our perspective upon what else a body can do?

## From body technology to embodied technology

Every technology serves the body in one way or another, from a pencil to a personal computer. A refrigerator or an oven facilitates human nutrition. Mobile phones and other personal digital devices link our bodies to a world of knowledge and communication, on the move, day and night. A rocket that can land on the moon extends the limits of human exploration, as does a submarine or a bicycle. The grim technologies of guns, bombs and nuclear weapons enable death and destruction to be dealt out impersonally. Technologies extend what a body can do, literally.

One of the earliest technologies that humans harnessed

must have been fire. Naturally occurring fires might have driven game into the arms of hunters, but would soon have been tamed to clear forests to make space for agriculture; to keep the body warm at night and deter wild animals; to cook; to fire clay pots and smelt metals; or to set off explosive charges in weaponry: fire is indeed a versatile servant of humans. Among the material technologies discovered, flint axes and arrow heads, cooking pots and vessels to store and transport liquids and foodstuffs give a sense of what prehistoric life was like. These early technologies provided human bodies with the fundamental needs of survival. Apart from objects intended purely for artistic purposes or bodily display, the 'material culture' found in museums of anthropology and archaeology comprise these technologies that humans developed over the millennia to aid their daily lives.

Technology is a cultural product, created by bodies to serve bodies. We may read in any technology-object both the purpose for which it is intended and the creative actions that have led to its development (Gordo Lopez and Cleminson 2004: 11; Lehoux et al. 2004: 620). Thinking back to chapter 5, technology-objects reflect the desires of their creators, be that a desire for warmth, for appetising food, for transport, or any other use to which a technology may be put. Over time, the sophistication of technology has increased, and one technology (for instance, the manufacture of steel or the development of electronics) has been used to make further technologies, providing us with the range of objects which we use today to manipulate our environment, our bodies, and those of others.

Health care has used technologies for millennia. Prehistoric tools suggest that circumcision, surgery for bladder stones and trephining (drilling a hole to release pressure within the skull) were common surgical procedures (Ellis 2009), while museums of medical history show the progression of instruments and other medical technology to the present. Modern hospitals abound with pieces of technology, ranging from items of equipment such as scanners and X-ray technology, to the drips, syringes and dressings that staff use to treat patients. The practice of medicine and health care is inextricably woven with technology (Walters 1995: 338).

While much technology in the hospital or clinic is devoted to diagnostics or treatment of disease, many technologies have also been associated with health or bodily impairment, and will include everything from dentures or dental implants, through assistive devices such as screen readers for the visually impaired, to pharmaceutical and invasive interventions such as gene therapy and cosmetic surgery. In health policy research and health economics, the concept of a *health technology* is drawn very broadly, to cover the range of tools, materials and techniques that may be applied in pursuit of the diagnosis, care, treatment and management of patients. These include:

- medical diagnostic, monitoring and therapeutic devices;
- assistive, adaptive and rehabilitative technologies including medical equipment such as wheelchairs, contact lenses, implant technology and information and communication aids;
- therapeutic technologies such as intradermal, subcutaneous and intramuscular needle injections, chemotherapy, and dialysis;
- pharmaceutical compounds;
- surgical technologies, from setting a broken limb to organ transplantation, and including techniques such as laparoscopic (keyhole) surgery and reconstructive and aesthetic plastic surgery;
- behavioural therapeutic technologies;
- complementary therapies such as hypnosis, homoeopathy or acupuncture.

Over time, technology has got both bigger and smaller. Early technologies were domestic: cups and cooking pots, combs and buckles, arrows and spears. The industrial revolution spawned the grand technological achievements of bridges and ships, steam engines and motor cars. Humanity and its technologies have reached as far as the Moon and beyond. But in the same period, bodies and technology have become more and more intimately associated. Now technology can be used to improve and enhance the body itself, often from the inside. Biology and engineering have come together to create embodied or 'cyborg' technology, while nanotechnology has shrunk the tools used to heal the body to a molecular level.

## Cyborg technologies

In science fiction futures, cyborgs are part-human, part-machine creations, in whom the best and the worst of these constituents play out their narratives. In the twenty-first century we now live in an era of cyborgs, in which the integration of engineering with biology in medical technology and science has contributed to the functional capacities of the bio-body (Haraway 1991: 150). Modern medicine increasingly uses technology to re-make and re-model the body and behaviour, from botox injections that smooth facial wrinkles to pharmaceuticals that smooth the stresses of life. As products of human culture, cyborg technologies customize bio-bodies according to human desires, fusing nature and culture within the body's skin. Many body technologies reflect the desire for health, the desire to overcome disease, and to resist ageing and death. As I write, yet another advance in genomic medicine has been heralded as the key to anti-ageing and the extension of the human life-span (there is a similar announcement every few weeks). Integration of technology offers possibilities for further steps in body evolution, but engineered by humanity, not by adaptation to the environment.

Cyborg technologies are not new: the Romans invented wooden false teeth and artificial limbs, and glass lenses to aid reading were developed in Arabic culture 1,000 years ago. Mary Shelley's tale of Dr Frankenstein and his monstrous but tragic creation predicted a future in which science would take apart and re-assemble human bodies piece by piece, aspiring to know the secrets of life itself. However, it is in the past century that engineering and biology have become more intimately associated, as scientific and technological expertise has been turned towards bodies and their biological capacities. The current applications of body technology include:

- joint replacements, prosthetic devices and other aids to mobility;
- organ transplants, including artificial organs and xeno-transplantation (cross-species);
- use of surgical techniques: to remove or correct disease or defects; to reconstruct the body; or otherwise to modify face, teeth, eyes and body for aesthetic objectives;
- pharmaceutical modification of disease processes and 'lifestyle' conditions, including sleep and wakefulness, sexual function, behaviour (for instance, stress and Attention Deficit and Hyperactivity Disorder), body shape and weight;
- stem cell and gene treatments to address degenerative diseases;
- reproductive technologies to both prevent and aid conception; and
- assistive technologies to overcome sensory impairments to vision, hearing or speech, including information technology applications.

Cyborgs from Frankenstein's monster to the benign *Star Trek* android Data have populated literature, films and TV. Yet the cyborg body of modern medicine is not the *Terminator* or the *Million Dollar Man*, a body imbued with superhuman strength. Typically, the cyborg of today's medicine is a relative weakling, a body that can do no more than match the capacities of the fully biological body, if that. Finally that is about to change. Body technology can be used not only to return a body to 'normal' function, but to enhance it beyond these norms. New technologies could be about to establish a body that really can push the limits. Fuller (2011) speaks of a future 'humanity 2.0' and the 'transhuman', in which information technology and artificial intelligence, nanotechnology and replacement body parts will free humans from their physical bodies. Technologies are blurring the beginning and end of biological life: new reproductive technologies have made 'test-tube babies' commonplace, while prenatal genetic testing, gene manipulation and cloning will shape human bodies in the future. Cryonics can freeze the dead, opening possibilities for future resurrection, while advances in artificial organs and even the integration of biological nerve cells with electronics could free humans from biology altogether. The melding of bodies with technology may finally confirm the Deleuzian view that 'life' is actually located within assemblages, rather than exclusively within organic bodies.

The prospect of body enhancement through pharmaceuticals has haunted competitive sport for the past fifty years, where use of steroids and other compounds is regarded as 'unfair' to athletes who depend upon 'natural' bodies enhanced only by exercise, nutrition and training. Now it is debated whether sprinter Oscar Pistorius' carbon-fibre lower limbs give him an advantage over athletes with biological ankles, while an Olympic marathon winner could not compete against a wheelchair-bound Paralympian equivalent. Viagra, a breakthrough treatment for erectile dysfunction, can give a male body a non-stop erection for 24 hours or more, a characteristic exploited (typically by fit young adults) to achieve extremes of sexual performance (Fox and Ward 2006). Gene therapies offer the promise of bodies afforded in-built protection from infectious and degenerative diseases.

What is driving these moves towards cyborg technology and what might be the consequences for bodies and identities?

## Science, technology and consuming bodies

There are four main motivators behind the emergence of cyborg technologies within modern culture. First, medical technologies have been developed in response to biomedicine's desires to provide better and better treatments to address inherited conditions, disease, accidents and battlefield injuries. The medical professions have created a demand for treatments and technologies, for example, to fashion replacements for damaged tissues, techniques to replace malfunctioning organs with human or animal transplants, 'test-tube' reproductive technologies to address fertility problems, and interventions at the molecular level with therapeutics and gene therapies. Biomedicine's minute dissection of body and disease processes drives this demand for body technology. More and more 'problems of daily life' such as shyness or hair loss have become a focus for medical attention, transforming aspects of life into diseases (Fishman 2004; Lexchin 2001).

Second, science and engineering expertise have been applied to biological processes over the past 100 years. Assistive devices such as hearing aids, dentures and wheelchairs marked a first phase in body technology, in which devices were intimately associated with bodies, but remained separate. Advances in engineering and materials have opened the prospect of integrating organic bodies and non-organic technology, for example through joint replacements, artificial hearts and corneal and cochlear implants to remedy visual and hearing impairments. New insights in biochemistry, immunology and genetics enable pharmaceuticals and gene therapies to be tailored to interact with the body's molecular processes. Computer science provided a further technological advance that heralded the possibility of cybernetic control of body tissues or prostheses, for instance, to enable motor control of an artificial limb or sight perception from a digital camera. Finally, nanotechnology miniaturizes technologies, allowing interaction with the body at a molecular level, for example enabling targeted delivery of drugs to specific tissues.

The third driver of body technologies is the economic and political context that has supported the industrial development of technologies, including pharmaceuticals, gene therapies and assistive devices. Most body technologies are produced commercially by private business. The pharmaceutical industry is the most profitable sector of commerce, with a global market for prescription drugs worth around $700 billion in 2010, and growing year-on-year (Henry and Lexchin 2002).

The major providers of body and cyborg technology (particularly in the pharmaceutical sector) are now multi-national, promoting their products in a globalized marketplace, and increasingly marketing directly to consumers. In 2005, the drugs with the biggest marketing budgets were a sleeping aid, a heartburn drug, two cholesterol-lowering pharmaceuticals and an asthma drug. Lifestyle drugs such as Viagra (sildenafil) have contributed significantly to drug company profits. In 2006, sales of Viagra netted $1.7 billion per year for its manufacturer.

Globally, consumers spend $12 billion each year on cosmetic surgery, and $1.5 billion on 'anti-ageing' creams (Fox and Ward 2008a). Consumerism is the final driver behind body technology. Sociologists have suggested that somewhere during the early twentieth century, Western society changed its focus from production to consumption (Featherstone 1991). Mass consumption was to be the engine of economic growth, whereas throughout previous human history the majority of people lived in relative or absolute poverty, with little access to any but the basics of existence. To feed this new emphasis on consumption, society required not only a population wealthy enough to consume, but also the desire for the goods produced.

Some products fulfil genuine need (for example, a drug to treat a disease or control pain), others, such as an all-in-one shower gel and shampoo, may not. For the latter, marketing must generate need, even if it did not exist prior to the product's creation. Successful marketing establishes objects of desire, so consumers come to believe a new hair product, a diet plan or a game console really will transform our experiences of life, love and happiness! Marketing emphasizes consumer goods' relations to bodies, from foods to clothes and hygiene products, to personal gadgets, to labour-saving domestic devices and other accoutrements of home comfort, to cars and even houses. Bodies can be preened and beautified, cosseted and pleased, eased and satisfied by consumption, according to the blurb on the packaging. Advertising becomes

> the guardian of the new morality, enticing individuals to participate in the consumption of commodities . . . Images of youth, beauty, luxury and opulence became loosely associated with goods, awakening long-suppressed desires (Featherstone 1991: 172)

For a successful consumer culture, desire must be channelled toward commodities, to make them objects of desire, regardless of intrinsic value. These include services (everything from a taxi ride to a lap dance) and artistic productions (including films and music), but technologies form the greater component of these objects. Traditionally, consumer technologies were cars, household goods, electronics, food and drink, beauty and cosmetic products, and entertainment media such as DVDs and music players. But increasingly, health, body and cyborg technologies are also targets for mass consumption. Cyborg technologies such as laser eye surgery, hair implants, teeth whitening and lifestyle pharmaceuticals are advertised on TV and in the media, often appealing to ideas of youth and beauty as selling-points. In countries such as the US and New Zealand that permit direct marketing to consumers, advertising extends to pharmaceutical products. The manufacturers of Viagra and rival compounds have all used popular sporting figures to front their marketing campaigns, re-focusing the product away from erectile dysfunction toward a younger market of men who want 'to improve the quality or duration of their erections' (Newman 2006: 12).

These four drivers contribute to technology assemblages as they interact with bodies. In the next section I want to look at how these factors: medical knowledge of the body; scientific and engineering innovation; the commercial basis of technology development; and the emergence of consumerism interact, with positive and negative consequences for embodiment and for identity.

## Bodies, technology assemblages and identity

As I noted earlier, all technologies reflect the desires of their creators. A drinking glass, an arrow, and a hypodermic syringe encapsulate the intentions behind their invention, and these desires are passed on to their users. This means that technology-objects have the potential to territorialize their users into certain behaviours. In the case of a glass, this territorialization is trivial: the technology supplies a vessel to hold liquids, usually to be imbibed, and consumers are encouraged to drink in standardizing quantities: 125ml for a glass of wine or a pint or half-litre for beer. The territorialization is minimal: we can use a glass to hold water, or petrol or even rice. If we don't like it, we can smash it!

Other technologies may territorialize more significantly. Consider the example of the metered-dose inhaler (MDI): a technology that millions of asthma sufferers use to self-manage their condition (Prout 1996). This device has been designed to provide a small dose of bronchodilator into the lungs before or at the beginning of an asthma attack, without an overdose that might cause dangerous side-effects, including heart arrhythmia. Prout suggests that the MDI 'stands in' for medical expertise, allowing patients to self-medicate, but at the same time retaining control by health professionals over the level of medication:

> Control over the drug . . . was given up [by doctors], but in a way that attempted to limit user autonomy by the metering abilities of the MDI, which in turn encoded biomedical judgements, concerns and purposes (1996: 206)

Early versions of inhaler technology had limited fail-safes to prevent under- or overdosing, and users had to be trained by their doctors before they were allowed to access the technology (ibid.). Consequently, many doctors argued that the device was unsafe and should not be dispensed to patients. Refinements incorporated more sophisticated technology that ensured a dose was only released when a user took a breath, reducing the capacity of human bodies to intentionally or unintentionally misuse the inhaler. The medical expertise provided to users by training was thus replaced by aspects of the technology itself (ibid.: 212–13). Prout described this as the 're-configuring' of the body by inhaler technology (ibid.: 214). This is the process that throughout this book has been called territorialization.

We can explore this example of the inhaler further. Every time a puff of bronchodilator is inhaled by a user's body, the MDI establishes relations to the intentions of its designer, and to medical knowledge and expertise in the treatment of asthma. There is an 'inhaler assemblage' here that includes these elements, along with the other relations that the user's body has with her/his experience of asthma and the medical profession. This assemblage territorializes the body: creating the likelihood that the disease can be self-managed effectively. It also establishes a subjectivity (or 'health identity') in the user as an 'asthma sufferer' who is co-operating with the medical profession to manage the symptoms effectively.

Every technology, to a greater or lesser extent, works like this. The body's relation to the technology will contribute to the body/technology assemblage, which in turn will affect the territorialization of the body (what it can do) and the health identity of the technology user. Consider another example, from Fox and Ward's (2008a) study of Viagra users. This is 'George', who was suffering from erectile dysfunction.

> My best friend at the office introduced me to Viagra a week after he saw my attitude change at the office due to my notice-able depression. Thanks to Viagra, I felt I am gaining my manhood again, but now lazy of doing sex without the blue pill. I am now becoming a big fan of Viagra, and afraid of having sex without Viagra.

George's body has been territorialized by his condition, but the drug has enabled a de-territorialization, so he feels he is 'gaining his manhood again'. However, the Viagra assemblage has also re-territorialized the body, so George now sees himself as dependent on Viagra. He has a health identity that is no longer that of a sufferer, but of a patient dependent upon a pharmaceutical for his sexuality. Think about our health technologies such as a wheelchair or a preventive drug like a statin that lowers blood cholesterol, and how they de-territorialize and re-territorialize their users.

Cyborg technologies have great potential to become key elements in assemblages and territorialize bodies into specific health identities. Because they are linked so closely to the body and to desires for health, beauty, youth and so forth, and because they have invested within them the expertise of science and biomedicine, they are potent relations for a body. They have the capacity to affect, with little other input, 'what else a body can do', opening up possibilities and closing others down. Some of these relations may be associated simply with biology, others have broader psychological, social or ethical relations. What, for instance, might be the relations associated with a technology such as in vitro fertilization for infertility, or hormone replacement therapy to ameliorate menopause?

I will look now in greater detail at the effects of technology on bodies, exploring a particular body technology to consider how it contributes to the 'medicalization' of life.

## Technology and the medicalization of daily life

Ivan Illich, a radical 1970s social philosopher, first argued that the medical profession was medicalizing parts of life such as childbirth and dying, making them into medical problems to be addressed by biomedicine, rather than fundamentals of life itself (Illich 1976). The view that modern medicine has gradually colonized more and more aspects of bodies is now well-established. Many aspects of women's bodies and their reproductive capacities, including conception, menstruation and the menopause, have been medicalized, according to Ehrenreich and English (2005). Conrad, who first explored the medicalization of hyperactivity in children in the 1970s, has recently described how adult hyperactivity, 'andropause' (a postulated equivalent to menopause in men), male pattern baldness and erectile dysfunction are now seen as medical conditions (Conrad 2007). Even sleep has been medicalized, say Williams et al. (2008), with insomnia, 'restless legs syndrome' and snoring all candidates to be regarded as diseases.

Medicalization occurs when

> a problem is defined in medical terms, described in medical language, understood by the adoption of a medical framework, or 'treated' with a medical intervention (Conrad 2007: 6)

When the concept was first established, the driver behind medicalization was believed to be efforts by the medical profession to achieve dominance over patients, or alternatively a generalized desire in a capitalist society to achieve control over the population (Ehrenreich 1978). Conrad, like other writers such as Fox and Ward (2008a) and Williams et al. (2008), argue that medicalization may now be a consequence of factors broader than medical dominance, and have identified the part that medical technologies play in the relentless medicalization of life.

As we have already seen in this chapter, technologies (such as asthma inhalers) are invested with the desires of their designers and promoters. But technologies are also the products of wider social, cultural and political contexts (Gordo Lopez and Cleminson 2004: 11; Fox 2011), and it is these other relations carried by a technology-object that may make them agents of medicalization. To explore these processes, I want to look at a specific example of body technology: lifestyle pharmaceutical products.

'Lifestyle' pharmaceuticals are those intended or used for

a purpose that 'falls into the border zone between the medical and social definitions of health' (such as male hair loss or erectile dysfunction), and those that 'treat diseases that derive from a person's lifestyle choices' (for example, obesity or nicotine addiction) (Lexchin 2001: 1449). These compounds are focused less on curing disease and more on enhancing people's quality of life. Some, such as sildenafil (Viagra) and the weight-loss drug orlistat (Xenical), were designed and manufactured to serve a lifestyle purpose, while others were created for one clinical use but also provided a secondary lifestyle use (Flower 2004: 182). For example, an anti-hypertensive drug and one developed to treat prostate disease are now marketed as effective treatments for male hair loss (androgenic alopecia). Other drugs marketed and prescribed for a non-lifestyle use find a different, lifestyle purpose among consumers. For instance, the drug norethisterone, usually prescribed as a contraceptive, hormone replacement therapy or to prevent menorrhagia (heavy menstrual bleeding), is increasingly requested by women in order to avoid inconvenient menstruation during holidays or other occasions (Shakespeare et al. 2000).

Many lifestyle drugs depend for their commercial success on creating consumer demand, with users transformed from recipients of medical care to 'active consumers of the latest pharmaceuticals' (Applbaum 2006: 446). In this new era of consumerism,

> it is both the responsibility and the entitlement of the consumer/patient to find paths to better health ... through information gathering and through responsible consumption practices (Fishman 2004: 202)

Marshall (2002: 133) argues that while drugs such as Viagra have been accepted by health professionals as contributing to the 'natural sexual response cycle', a further element in their success is their acceptance by consumers as a 'magic bullet' that will revolutionize sexual relations by restoring normal functionality. The following extracts are from Fox and Ward's (2008a) research on lifestyle pharmaceuticals (all names are research pseudonyms). Richard had incorporated use of Viagra in his life, and accorded it significance for key aspects of his sexual relationship with his wife.

> I have ED all the time, as defined as the inability to achieve or maintain an erection. Does that mean do I always take a Viagra before I engage in sexual activity? No, I don't, because I engage my wife in some sort of sexual activity almost every day. She demands and deserves my physical attention. But when we want sustained intercourse, I take Viagra. That's maybe once or twice a week on average.

Similarly, users of the weight-loss medicine orlistat (Xenical, now also available as the pharmacy medicine Alli) had made the drug central to their diets, even though its main effect is simply to prevent fat uptake, not to control calories. Users of Xenical soon learn to restrict their fat intake, in order to avoid the unpleasant side-effect of diarrhoea. However, Elsie regarded the drug and not her own efforts to manage her diet as the basis for her weight loss.

> If you eat a regular diet, separate your carbs from your fats and proteins, eat one carb meal and choose only coloured vegetables with your meats. The body metabolizes better when you don't mix! I have also noticed that warm soups make Xenical work better. And fruit is a great additive too.

We can see elements of the medicalization and 'pharmaceuticalization' of sexuality and weight loss within these extracts, based on social norms for penetrative sex and body shape. The medicines reinforce these norms, and for these respondents, the drugs became a core element of what goes on in their bedrooms and kitchens, rather than something extraneous. Indeed, they regarded these pharmaceutical products as allies that enabled them to overcome the physical restrictions of erectile dysfunction or obesity. Furthermore, the drugs established a subjectivity or 'health identity' in each of these users as dependent upon the medication to resolve their problem of living.

This case study of lifestyle pharmaceuticals also demonstrates the four drivers behind cyborg technologies identified earlier, and how these contribute relations to the technology assemblage. First, there is a demand from the medical professions to find treatments for problems and conditions of the patients who consult them. Professionals may feel impotent to address problems at the limit of what might be called disease, and welcome new treatments to meet their patients' demands. Second, there is the emergence of new scientific discoveries that can be developed as treatments for lifestyle conditions such as over-weight, impotence and hair loss. Sometimes these discoveries are intentional, while others are serendipitous, as in the case of the drugs mentioned earlier that can be used in male pattern baldness. Thirdly, the profit-orientation of, and competitive marketplace inhabited by industries such as pharmaceutical companies drives the continual search for new compounds that can be developed for market, or adapted to a new use. Business success or failure will depend upon developing new technologies and generating new demand. Finally, the emergence of health consumerism fuels demand for effective treatments for problems and conditions, and creates a ready market for new products.

These four factors interact with each other in various ways as new technologies are developed. Pharmaceutical companies produce not only drugs but also the medico-scientific knowledge that justifies the product's value as the solution to a problem (Fishman 2004). Health technology companies are the largest funders of US medical research (Lexchin 2001), and commission and fund academic scientists and clinicians to undertake trials of their compounds, to provide credibility to findings. Drugs such as Viagra were promoted 'through scientific claims about the medical benefit, efficacy and necessity, supposedly revealed by objective clinical research' (Fishman 2004: 189).

Health technology companies devote huge sums to marketing their products to the medical professions, with teams of sales reps touring hospitals with the hope of persuading clinicians to adopt a new treatment. Direct-to-consumer (DTC) marketing has also grown in the US and New Zealand, as was noted earlier. In Europe and Australia, where DTC marketing is illegal, manufacturers may seek other approaches. In the UK, pharmaceutical companies work closely with and fund patient pressure-groups such as cancer and Alzheimer's disease charities, who in turn lobby government to get specific drugs funded by the NHS (Fox et al. 2005c). Decisions by a government to approve or even fund a product may be key to the commercial future of a health technology producer.

In the US, a drug can only gain Food and Drugs Administration (FDA) approval if it treats an established 'disease' (Fishman 2004: 192), and consequently there will be strong efforts by manufacturers to medicalize lifestyle conditions. In the UK, Viagra and similar medicines are only available on NHS prescription for men whose erectile dysfunction is due to an underlying medical condition, or causes them 'severe psychological distress' (Sairam et al. 2002). Xenical may be prescribed for those defined as overweight or obese patients by body-mass index, but eligible patients must first have begun dietary, exercise and behavioural programmes to reduce weight (NICE 2006).

Oddly, sometimes the emergence of an effective treatment may tip a body condition into a disease. This was the case with the medical-sounding *erectile dysfunction*, which prior to Viagra's launch was commonly known as *male impotence*, a term implying weakness (Newman 2006: 5). Shyness has morphed into 'social phobia', to be treated with Seroxat (Lexchin 2001), while the development of Ritalin may have hastened the acceptance of Attention Deficit Hyperactivity Disorder as a disease (Fishman 2004). With an effective drug treatment now available for androgenic alopecia (male pattern baldness: a secondary sexual characteristic), the stigma associated with the condition may be medicalized as a psychiatric pathology such as 'body dysmorphic disorder' (Cash 2001: 163).

So we can see a complex web of relations build around a health technology such as a lifestyle pharmaceutical. This means that the technology is never 'just' technology: social, political and economic relations are built into something as apparently trivial as a Viagra pill. These relations are carried with the technology, contributing to the assemblage on the bodies of all those who use it (both as providers and consumers), and territorializing the body in this way or that. This in turn can affect the health identity of the technology's user.

Cyborg technologies are particularly potent transmitters of social relations because they are so intimately involved, not only with the biology of the body, but also with psychological and social aspects of embodiment (for instance, a desire, an aspiration or a fear; dependency or independence). But any technology; a pill, a surgical procedure or a piece of equipment may have these effects, to a greater or lesser extent, depending upon the particular contexts of a body. What, for example, might be the impact of an ultrasound scan for a pregnant woman and her partner, or the effect of results from an MRI scan for someone with a suspected brain tumour? However, as we have seen throughout this book, there is nothing deterministic about body relations. So when do technologies territorialize bodies, and how may this territorialization be resisted?

## Technology and the politics of the body

Health technologies are often cast as either heroes or villains. In popular media, a new health technology advance or 'breakthrough' seems to be a daily occurrence. Gene therapies, cancer cures, new reproductive technologies, stem cells all seem to offer new hope and expectations for the future. On the other hand, health technologies can be criticized for creating hazards (Anonymous 2010), for restricting what patient-users can do (Lehoux et al. 2004), or for de-humanizing care or de-skilling. Daly (1989) criticized echocardiography as a diagnostic tool for creating high levels of anxiety among patients. Nurses who had embraced technology when first introduced into critical care units later judged it 'disruptive and dangerous', turning them into little more than technicians caring for machines rather than patients (Sandelowski 1997). These responses to technology and its power or control over bodies can be called the 'politics of the body'.

Generally speaking, those who herald great technological advances see technology as 'neutral' ('just technology'), while those who see pitfalls in technology regard it as value-laden, having a (usually negative) social influence over those involved (Feenberg 1999: 2). But this analysis of technology in health care is too simplistic: we cannot easily judge a specific technology as good or evil, neutral or determining. Empirical studies have shown that some patients found a health technology controlling or enslaving, while others in similar circumstances have subverted the same technology, using it to their own ends (Lehoux et al. 2004: 640).

What the earlier case study of lifestyle pharmaceuticals showed is that a technology may indeed territorialize the bodies of its users, but that the shape of this territorialization will vary from individual to individual, depending upon the broader sets of relations that a body has, and how these limit or enable what else it can do. In the extracts from users of lifestyle drugs, we saw the active engagement of bodies with the technology, not some kind of passive submission to the products and their effects. Importantly, this suggests that bodies cannot simply be controlled by technology, any more than they can by other powerful forces. Bodies have the capacity to *resist* territorialization and constantly exercise this capacity. Let's look at this in greater detail.

Earlier I showed, using the example of the asthma inhaler, how technologies incorporate the original desires of their inventors and developers. Prout's (1996) study of the metered dose inhaler (MDI) demonstrated how biomedical expertise can be built into a technology-object, to control how it can be used, principally to render it safe. What kinds of territorialization of the user's body occur with this technology? Firstly, there is a physical territorialization: the bronchodilator drug in the inhaler will have a pharmacological effect on the tissues of the user's body, de-territorializing the user's body from the biological effects of an asthma flare-up. There is also territorialization that goes with the need to use the inhaler in a designated way, and at appropriate times when symptoms indicate the onset of an asthma episode. The inhaler must be carried with the user at all times in order to allow the user to self-manage the condition.

Other territorializations are less predictable. Use of the inhaler before exercise can remove some of the physical limitations that asthma can impose on a sufferer (Villaran et al. 1999). Possession of the MDI may also provide psychological reassurance to the user, or it may create anxiety over the unpredictability of an episode. The user may feel stigma associated with having an object that declares to others that s/he is an asthma sufferer, or may feel inhibited in taking physical or sporting exercise because of the need to carry the inhaler, or because it reminds the user of the risks of having an asthma episode. Alternatively, the user might feel liberated, because s/he can self-manage her condition, with only infrequent need to consult with a professional.

The reason for the indeterminate effect of an inhaler on the body is that the technology-object itself is only one element in a more complex assemblage on the body of the user. The relations comprising this assemblage will include

lungs – asthma – inhaler – biomedicine

but will also involve all sorts of other relations particular to the individual body. These might include relations to family and friends, to fears and anxieties resulting from knowledge or experience of asthma episodes, involvement in activities, and personal commitments and aspirations. As with other assemblages discussed in this book, the possibilities are endless!

It is thus the particular shape of the assemblage that will influence the effect on what else a body can do, rather than the technology-object itself. This variability in the 'inhaler-assemblage' means that we cannot predict the effects of the technology on an individual, without knowing a great deal about the context within which the technology is used. Nor will a technology directly affect a user's health identity: again this is shaped by the overall body and health assemblages, and by the active, experimenting creativity of the body itself (see chapter 5).

The analysis of the four drivers behind cyborg technologies such as lifestyle drugs suggests what kinds of relations may be associated with a technology. We saw how technologies are driven by the medical professions; by scientific expertise; by the economic and commercial interests behind technologies and by consumerism. A technology will be located within a framework of relations to these elements, and the effect of a technology on a body and on a health identity will depend upon how these four factors relate to, and affect a user's body. The technology does not, in itself, determine how a user's body is affected.

This can be illustrated by looking at examples in which body technologies are used in ways not intended by their inventors, developers, or professionals who apply them. For instance, we have already seen how norethisterone, prescribed as a contraceptive, hormone replacement therapy or for heavy menstrual bleeding, is requested by women to suppress menstruation at inconvenient times (Shakespeare et al. 2000). Another example is recreational use of Viagra, often by males and females who from a medical point of view would not be considered to be sexually dysfunctional. A study found it was used for marathon sex sessions; so a gay male could experience sex with a female friend; or by women to enhance their sexual experiences (Fox and Ward 2006: 468–70). Most remarkably, prescription weight-loss drugs were used by young people with anorexia to sustain extremely low body mass (ibid.: 473).

These 'transgressive' uses of health technologies suggest that they may be used specifically to *resist* territorialization. These users certainly do not adhere to a medical model of health and illness, and by challenging medical authority and scientific knowledge, they forge a health identity in opposition to 'patient' or 'dependency'. At the same time, they may have adopted a consumer mentality towards technology (as noted earlier, pharmaceutical companies have themselves seen new markets among healthy users of Viagra and similar products, and have capitalized on this non-medical, transgressive use of their compounds). Fox and Ward (2006) suggest that these 'resisting consumers' represent a health identity that is intended to de-territorialize embodiment, opening up new possibilities for what a body can do. Technology can always be subverted to fulfil or facilitate the desires of the creative, experimenting body.

## Conclusion: bodies and the technology assemblage

In this final chapter, I have looked at how bodies use technologies, in particular health technologies, to enhance their capacities. Cyborg technologies, those that are more and more intimately tied to the body, offer some new opportunities for the body to transcend its limitations, to open up possibilities for action. These technologies offer the potential for bodies not only to resist the effects of disease and ageing, but perhaps also to overcome the limitations of biology. At the same time, these technologies can be powerful sources of territorialization, establishing dependencies in their users, and health identities in which more and more aspects of daily life become medicalized. Yet it is always possible for a body to resist territorialization, and it may even use technology as an ally to achieve a line of flight.

Think once again about Alice Martin, the older adult who suffers from osteoarthritis, whom we have met throughout this book. Alice has used many health technologies throughout her life, from self-medication with painkillers or other over-the-counter medicines, to stronger analgesics during childbirth. Perhaps her delivery required the use of an epidural anaesthetic, or needed forceps or other instruments. Her routine visits to the doctor's may also have involved technologies, to check blood pressure, pulse, or more complex therapies or diagnostics. The onset of arthritis will have brought Alice into secondary care, and technologies from painkillers and anti-inflammatories through to her knee replacement. Alice is now a cyborg!

For Alice, health technologies have been important to sustain her quality of life, and reduce the effects of disease. They have de-territorialized her body from the limiting effects of arthritis, opening up possibilities for what her body can do. Yet at the same time these technologies have imposed an assemblage on her body in which the norms and values of biomedicine, the social expectations surrounding a 75-year-old female body, the commercial interests of technology manufacturers and the economics of health care delivery are all present. Alice has been medicalized by these technologies and she has a health identity as a patient, with all that entails (see chapter 4).

This territorialization as patient can weigh heavily, as it renders the body passive, and always to be compared negatively with a 'healthy' body, and as a reminder of future degeneration and eventual death. Yet Alice is not a victim, she is able to resist, and the kinds of support we looked at in the chapter on care may help her to find new possibilities for action and identity, for instance by working as a volunteer for the arthritis charity she supports. Health technologies shape her body, but within much broader assemblages of living that we have looked at throughout this book.

For health care professionals, technology is a part of daily life, and like them or loathe them, modern medicine relies heavily upon technologies. Body and cyborg technologies are becoming more and more widely applied within health care as new advances in bio-technology, nanotechnology and cybernetics integrate bodies and technology ever more closely. This means that in an interaction between professional and patient, technology may frequently be a third party. Sometimes patients almost disappear under the technology (literally or metaphorically), and professionals must make sure that their primary allegiance is to the patient, not to the mass of beeping kit that monitors, sustains and treats the patient's body. In this way, technology can be the tool, not the master in the care of bodies.

### Suggested further reading

Fox, N. J. and Ward, K. J. (2008) Pharma in the bedroom . . . and the kitchen. The pharmaceuticalization of daily life. *Sociology of Health and Illness*, 30 (6), 856–68.

Fuller, S. (2011) *Humanity 2.0: The Past, Present and Future of What It Means to Be Human*. London: Palgrave Macmillan.

Prout, A. (1996) Actor-network theory, technology and medical sociology: an illustrative analysis of the metered dose inhaler. *Sociology of Health and Illness*, 18 (2), 198–219.

# Conclusion

In the first two chapters of this book, I described two rival histories of the body: the natural and social bodies that scientists, social scientists and philosophers have researched, explored and explained over the past two millennia. These histories demonstrate how the body has been 'claimed' by biology and social science, and created in the images of these disciplines. For biology, the body is composed of organic material, with more and more aspects of life, behaviour and human culture explicable by biological process. For social science, the body is the outcome of human culture, and just happens to be based on a biological frame.

In the rest of the book, I argued that making this kind of distinction between a biological body and a social body is not helpful. In particular, health and social care professionals need to recognize that the body is always both natural and social, and that these aspects are intertwined: in health and illness; in the desires of the body for nutrition and sexuality; in how bodies are managed in health care; in how professionals care for bodies; and how bodies and technology are increasingly intertwined.

Bodies are surrounded with other bodies and objects, from birth to death and beyond. They are always in relationship to these others, and they affect and are affected by their relations. To understand the body, we need to think of it always within networks of relationship. What relations a body has determines not what it *is*, but what (else) it can *do*. In other words, what is a body's potential, what are its capacities for future action, and what are the limits on what it can do? Relations can be material, psychological, social, economic, political and philosophical. In general, the more relations a body has, the more it can do.

Alongside this understanding of a relational body that can do this or that, a parallel theme ran through the book. The Deleuzian perspective on the body emphasizes the active, creative, experimenting character of the body. The body is not a passive vessel waiting to be filled by experience, passing through phases of growth, maturity and ageing, shaped by forces beyond its control. Rather, it is always in the act of making its own history, reaching out, testing limits, trying something new, admitting or refusing the possibilities it encounters.

What do these two fundamentals of the body – as relational and as creative and engaged – mean for health and social care, for care professionals, and indeed for anyone with a body? I shall summarize this by recalling the case study I have used from time to time in this book, the older adult Mrs Alice Martin. Alice, you will recall, is 75 and suffers from osteoarthritis. I will make five concluding points.

First, despite her degenerative disease, Alice's body has many relations, and can do many things because of these relationships. These relations are the consequence of a lifetime of experiences; every encounter with an object, another body or an idea has left a trace. Those that have affected Alice the most, for example through habitual contact, emotional intensity or impact on her life or her body, will have the greatest effect, while others may now be little more than memories, or even have withered away altogether. Alice herself may not actually be aware of some of her body's relations: for instance to the social, economic and political processes that organize many of society's institutions and formations (for instance, the economics of drug manufacture or the gender mix of the caring professions). Human bodies have far more relations than those of other animals, as a consequence of their capacities to affect and be affected by cultural products and ideas. This provides humans with such extensive capacities, meaning that, in comparison with a cat or a crab or a caterpillar, their bodies can do so much else.

The relations that affect Alice come together to create *assemblages*, linking Alice's body to the social and natural environments (Bogue 1989: 91), and creating the substrate (the *body-without-organs*) that both defines a person's capacities and her/his limits. Assemblages are like machines: they do something. There is perhaps a family assemblage, linking Alice to family members (alive and dead) through ideas of love, loyalty, responsibility and care. There may be a belonging assemblage that locates Alice's body within a space that is both geographical and psychological/emotional. There will certainly be an osteoarthritis assemblage, which will comprise not only relations to the disease, but also to the medical professions, to her lay and professional carers and to Alice's involvement in an osteoarthritis charity. There will be a sexuality assemblage, an ageing assemblage, and others too. Health and social care professionals must recognize the web of relations that link bodies to their physical and social environment, often independent of health, illness and disease.

Second, these assemblages, confluent with the active, desiring and experimenting creativity of Alice's body, territorialize her, and set the limits on what (else) her body can do. While arthritis may impose some limitations on her physical functions, these limits also derive from her own and others' expectations of what a 75-year-old can (and should) do; her social position as a patient dependent on professional knowledge, expertise and allocation of resources; her economic circumstances; her family and networks of friends, and so forth. Professionals may play a key role in the assemblages of their patients and clients, and need to recognize the strength and extent of their impact on their bodies, sometimes in ways they may not realize.

Third, if the body is territorialized by its assemblages, then it is also de-territorialized by them. Assemblages may counter each other, so that a family assemblage may counteract the effects of a biomedicine assemblage. A single new relation can affect the body in this way, leading to de-territorialization. We looked at the role of care in this way, in chapter 7. Alice may gain support, encouragement and new opportunities from a carer (be it a family member, friend or professional) that can counter the limits on the body imposed by disease, ageing or expectations. It can take very little effort to achieve this: perhaps a moment of connection as an equal, rather than professional distance, may be all it needs to de-territorialize the body of a care recipient.

Fourth, the assemblages on Alice's body also determine her identity or sense of herself. We saw in chapter 3 how the sense we have of ourselves (and our capacity to reflect on who we are and what we wish to become) emerges gradually during childhood and into adult life from a myriad of possible identities, as a consequence of our relations to the world around us. Humans have the capacity to reflect and apply concepts to ourselves, as we can to other things and bodies. For Alice, her sense of herself has matured as relations have accrued and resulting assemblages shaped what her body can do. Institutions such as school and the workplace will have contributed, as will the gender assigned to her, and her roles as a wife and a mother. Health and illness also contribute to identity, and more recently the onset of a chronic identity will have affected her sense of who she is, and what she can do. Biomedicine has a part to play in her health identity too: relations with health professionals often shape identity towards passive 'patienthood'. But Alice is active in her response to osteoarthritis; she has become an expert in managing her condition, and works with health and social care professionals as an equal partner. Ageing too brings a challenge to identity, and helping people to resist the territorialization of ageing can be an important part of sustaining 'health', which can be seen as a 'line of flight' from the territorializations of illness, dependency and limitation.

Finally, for Alice (as with us all), modern life has surrounded her body with technology, from the clothes she wears and tools she uses to cook and eat, to the TV and digital devices that make life enjoyable, to the health and body technologies of modern medicine that we saw in chapter 8. Old age and chronic illness have brought body technology into Alice's life. She had a knee replacement five years ago, and may get more cyborg joint replacements in the future. Every day, pharmaceutical technology eases the pain of her condition. Body technologies can de-territorialize bodies from the effects of disease and pain, yet as we saw, they carry within them the intentions of their designers, so they territorialize and shape bodies at the same time. Our bodies have become an element within technology assemblages; we are all a mix of organic and inorganic matter. Care professionals can ensure technology is the servant not the master of the body.

So Alice and her body, as with every one of us, is part of a life-long dance of relations. There is a 'politics' to embodiment, comprising the play of relations on the body, and how these affect us and are affected by us, how we are territorialized and how we resist. Health professionals perform a key role in this body politics, and can make all the difference to the physical, psychological and emotional experiences of embodiment of their patients and clients through their understanding of what else a body can do. Having a body is an extraordinary journey, shaped by the unique combinations of biological, psychological, social and philosophical relationships that bodies gain through their experiences, sensations and reflections. The human body always resides within a network of assemblages, along with other bodies, objects, ideas, social formations and technologies: part organic, part inorganic. This comprises the body-without-organs. On it

> we sleep, live our waking lives, fight – fight and are fought – seek our place, experience untold happiness and fabulous defeats, on it we penetrate and are penetrated, on it we love. (Deleuze and Guattari 1988: 150)

It's amazing.

# References

Abraham, J. (2010) Pharmaceuticalisation of society in context; theoretical, empirical and health dimensions. *Sociology*, 44 (4), 603–22.

Adam, B. (1990) *Time and Social Theory*. Cambridge: Polity.

Adkins, L. and Lury, C. (2000) Making bodies, making people, making work. In McKie, L. and Watson, N. (eds) *Organizing Bodies. Policy, Institutions and Work*. Basingstoke: Macmillan, pp. 151–65.

Anderson, B. M. (1991) Mapping the terrain of the discipline. In Gray, G. and Pratt, R. (eds) *Towards a Discipline of Nursing*. Melbourne: Churchill Livingstone.

Anonymous (2010) Top 10 health technology hazards for 2011. *Health Devices*, 39 (11), 386–98. Accessed at https://www.ecri.org/Forms/Pages/2011_Top_10_Technology_Hazards.aspx

Ansell Pearson, K. (1999) *Germinal Life*. London: Routledge.

Applbaum, K. (2006) Pharmaceutical marketing and the invention of the medical consumer. *PLoS Medicine*, 3 (4), 445–7.

Armstrong, D. (1983) *The Political Anatomy of the Body*. Cambridge: Cambridge University Press.

Arney, W. and Neill, J. (1982) The location of pain in childbirth, natural childbirth and the transformation of obstetrics. *Sociology of Health and Illness*, 4 (1), 1–24.

Ashton, J. and Seymour, H. (1988) *The New Public Health*. Buckingham: Open University Press.

Baumann, A. and Silverman, B. (1998) Deprofessionalization in health care; flattening the hierarchy. In Groarke, L. (ed.) *The Ethics of the New Economy: Restructuring and Beyond*. Waterloo, Ontario: Wilfrid Laurier University Press.

Beck, U. (1992) *Risk Society*. London: Sage.

(1994) The reinvention of politics: towards a theory of reflexive modernization. In Beck, U., Giddens, A. and Lash, S. (eds) *Reflexive Modernization*. Cambridge: Polity.

Berger, P. and Luckmann, T. (1991) *The Social Construction of Reality*. London: Penguin.

Bernasconi, O. (2010) Being decent, being authentic: the moral self in shifting discourses of sexuality across three generations of Chilean women. *Sociology*, 44 (5), 860–75.

Biggs, S. (1997) Choosing not to be old? Masks, bodies and identity management in later life. *Ageing and Society*, 17 (5): 553–70.

Bissell, P., May, C. and Noyce, P. (2004) From compliance to concordance: barriers to accomplishing a re-framed model of health care interactions. *Social Science and Medicine*, 58 (4), 851–62.

Bogue, R. (1989) *Deleuze and Guattari*. London: Routledge.

Bourdieu, P. (1984) *Distinction: A Social Critique of the Judgement of Taste*. London: Routledge.

Bourdieu, P. and Passeron, J.C. (1990) *Reproduction in Education, Society, and Culture*. London: Sage.

Brammall, K. M. (1996) Monstrous metamorphosis: nature, morality, and the rhetoric of monstrosity in Tudor England. *The Sixteenth Century Journal*, 27 (1), 3–21.

Brewis, J. (2000) 'When a body meets a body'. Experiencing the female body at work. In McKie, L. and Watson, N. (eds) *Organizing Bodies. Policy, Institutions and Work*. Basingstoke: Macmillan, pp. 166–84.

Brown, G. W. and Harris, T. (1978) *The Social Origins of Depression. A Study of Psychiatric Disorder in Women*. London: Tavistock Publications.

Buchanan, I. (1997) The problem of the body in Deleuze and Guattari, or, what can a body do? *Body and Society*, 3, 73–91.

Bunting, S. (1993) *Rosemarie Parse. Theory of Health as Human Becoming*. Newbury Park, CA: Sage.

Bunton, R. (1992) 'More than a woolly jumper': health promotion as social regulation. *Critical Public Health*, 3 (20), 4–11.

Butler, C., Rollnick, S. and Stott, N. (1996) The practitioner, the patient and resistance to change: recent ideas on compliance. *Canadian Medical Association Journal*, 154 (9), 1357–62.

Butler, J. (1990) *Gender Trouble*. London: Routledge.

Cacioppo, John T. and Hawkley, Louise C. (2003) Social isolation and health, with an emphasis on underlying mechanisms. *Perspectives in Biology and Medicine*, 46 (3), S39–52.

Cameron-Traub, E. (1991) An evolving discipline. In Gray, G. and Pratt, R. (eds) *Towards a Discipline of Nursing*. Melbourne: Churchill Livingstone.

Canguilhem, G. (1989) *The Normal and the Pathological*. New York: Zone Books.

Cash, T. F. (2001) The psychology of hair loss and its implications for patient care. *Clinics in Dermatology*, 19, 161–6.

Castells, M. (2004) *The Power of Identity*. Oxford: Blackwell.

Charmaz, K. (1983) Loss of self: a fundamental form of suffering in the chronically ill. *Sociology of Health and Illness*, 5, 168–95.

(1995) The body, identity, and self: adapting to impairment. *The Sociological Quarterly*, 36 (4), 657–80.

Chua, W.-F. and Clegg, S. (1990) Professional closure. The case of British nursing. *Theory and Society*, 19, 135–72.

Cixous, H. (1986) Sorties. In Cixous, H. and Clement, C. (eds) *The Newly Born Woman*. Manchester: Manchester University Press.

Clarke, A. E., Shim, J. K., Mamo, L., Fosket, J. R. and Fishman, J. R. (2003) Biomedicalization: technoscientific transformations of health, illness and US biomedicine. *American Sociological Review*, 68 (2), 161–94.

Clegg, Brian (2003) *The First Scientist: A Life of Roger Bacon*. London: Constable and Robinson.

Connolly, P. (1997) Racism and postmodernism: towards a theory of practice. In Owen, D. (ed.) *Sociology after Postmodernism*. London: Sage, pp. 65–80.

Conrad, P. (2007) *The Medicalization of Society*. Baltimore, MD: Johns Hopkins University Press.

Coulter, A. (2002) *The Autonomous Patient – Ending Paternalism in Medical Care*. London: Nuffield Trust.

Crossley, N. (1995) Merleau-Ponty, the elusive body and carnal sociology. *Body and Society*, 1 (1), 43–63.

Currier, D. (2003) Feminist technological futures: Deleuze and body/technology assemblages. *Feminist Theory*, 4 (3), 321–38.

Dalton, S. O., Boesen, E. H., Ross, L. et al. (2002) Mind and cancer: do psychological factors cause cancer? *European Journal of Cancer*, 38 (10), 1313–23.

Daly, J. (1989) Innocent murmurs: Echocardiography and the diagnosis of cardiac normality. *Sociology of Health and Illness*, 11 (2), 99–116.

Darke, G. (1996) Discourses on the menopause and female sexual identity. In Holland, J. and Adkins, L. (eds) *Sex, Sensibility and the Gendered Body*. Basingstoke: Palgrave Macmillan.

Darwin, C. (1859) *On the Origin of Species by Means of Natural Selection, or the Preservation of Favoured Races in the Struggle for Life*. London: John Murray.

Davey-Smith, G., Dorling, D., Mitchell, R. and Shaw, M. (2002) Health inequalities in Britain: continuing increases up to the end of the twentieth century. *Journal of Epidemiology and Community Health*, 56, 434–5.

de Swaan, A. (1990) *The Management of Normality*. London: Routledge.

Deacon, R. (2006) Michel Foucault on education: a preliminary theoretical overview. *South African Journal of Education*, 26 (2), 177–87.

Deleuze, G. and Guattari, F. (1984) *Anti-Oedipus: Capitalism and Schizophrenia*. London: Athlone.

(1988) *A Thousand Plateaus*. London: Athlone.

(1994) *What is Philosophy?* New York: Columbia University Press.

Department of Health (2001) *The Expert Patient: a New Approach to Chronic Disease Management for the 21st Century*. London: Department of Health.

Dolan, J. (1985) *Nursing in Society, an Historical Perspective*. Philadelphia: WB Saunders.

Dols, M. W. (1987) The origins of the Islamic hospital: myth and reality. *Bulletin of the History of Medicine*, 61 (3), 367–90.

Douglas, M. (1966) *Purity and Danger: An Analysis of Concepts of Pollution and Taboo*. London: Routledge.

(1996) *Natural Symbols*. London: Routledge.

Duff, C. (2010) Towards a developmental ethology: exploring Deleuze's contribution to the study of health and human development. *Health*, 14 (6), 619–34.

Duncombe, J. and Marsden, D. (1993) Love and intimacy: the gender division of emotion and 'emotion work': a neglected aspect of sociological discussion of heterosexual relationships. *Sociology*, 27 (2), 221–41.

Ehrenreich, J. (1978) Introduction. In Ehrenreich, J. (ed.) *The Cultural Crisis of Modern Medicine*. New York: Monthly Review Press.

Ehrenreich, B. and English, D. (2005) *For Her Own Good: Two Centuries of the Experts' Advice to Women*. New York: Anchor Books.

Eisenberg, L. (1977) Disease and illness. *Culture, Medicine and Psychiatry*, 1, 9–23.

Elias, N. (1991) On human beings and their emotions: a process-sociological essay. In Featherstone, M., Hepworth, M. and Turner, B. S. (eds) *The Body*. London: Sage, pp. 103–25.

(2000) *The Civilizing Process*. Oxford: Blackwell.

Ellis, H. (2009) *The Cambridge Illustrated History of Surgery*. Cambridge: Cambridge University Press.

Emerson, J. (1970) Behaviour in public places: sustaining definitions of reality in gynecological examinations. In Dreitzel, H. P. (ed.) *Recent Sociology 2*. New York: Macmillan.

Engel, G. L. (2008) The need for a new medical model: a challenge for biomedicine. *Science*, 196 (4286), 129–36.

Featherstone, M. (1991) The body in consumer culture. In

Featherstone, M., Hepworth, M. and Turner, B. S. (eds) *The Body*. London: Sage, pp. 170–96.

Featherstone, M. and Hepworth, M. (1982) Ageing and inequality: consumer culture and the new middle age. In Robbins, D., Day, G., Caldwell, L. et al. (eds) *Rethinking Social Inequality*. Aldershot: Gower.

Feenberg, A. (1999) *Questioning Technology*. London: Routledge.

Fisher, S. (1991) A discourse of the social: medical talk/power talk/oppositional talk? *Discourse and Society*, 2, 157–82.

Fishman, R. (2004) Manufacturing desire: the commodification of female sexual dysfunction. *Social Studies of Science*, 34 (2), 187–218.

Flower, R. (2004) Lifestyle drugs: pharmacology and the social agenda. *Trends in Pharmacological Sciences*, 25 (4), 182–5.

Ford, C. A. (1996) A theory of individual creative action in multiple social domains. *Academy of Management Review*, 21 (4), 1112–42.

Foucault, M. (1970) *The Order of Things. An Archaeology of the Human Sciences*. London: Tavistock.

(1971) *Madness and Civilisation. A History of Insanity in the Age of Reason*. London: Tavistock.

(1976) *The Birth of the Clinic*. London: Tavistock.

(1979) *Discipline and Punish*. Harmondsworth: Peregrine.

(1980) The eye of power. In Gordon, C. (ed.) *Power/Knowledge*. Brighton: Harvester.

(1984) *The History of Sexuality Vol. 1: The Will to Knowledge*. Harmondsworth: Penguin.

(1985) *The Use of Pleasure (Vol. 2 of the History of Sexuality)*. New York: Pantheon.

(1986) *The Care of the Self (Vol. 3 of the History of Sexuality)*. New York: Pantheon.

(2002) *The Archaeology of Knowledge*. London: Routledge.

Fox, N. J. (1993) *Postmodernism, Sociology and Health*. Buckingham: Open University Press.

(1995) Postmodern perspectives on care: the Vigil and the Gift. *Critical Social Policy*, 15 (44–5), 107–24.

(1998) Foucault, Foucauldians and sociology. *British Journal of Sociology*, 49 (3), 415–33.

(1999) *Beyond Health. Postmodernism and Embodiment*. London: Free Association Books.

(2002a) Refracting health: Deleuze, Guattari and body/self. *Health*, 6 (1), 347–64.

(2002b) What a 'risky' body can do: Why people's health choices are not all based in evidence. *Health Education Journal*, 61 (2), 166–79.

(2005) Cultures of ageing in Thailand and Australia (what can an ageing body do?) *Sociology*, 39 (3), 501–18.

(2011) Boundary objects, social meanings and the success of new technologies. *Sociology*, 45 (1), 70–85.

Fox, N. J. and Ward, K. J. (2006) Health identities: from expert patient to resisting consumer. *Health*, 10 (4), 461–79.

(2008a) Pharma in the bedroom . . . and the kitchen. The pharmaceuticalisation of daily life. *Sociology of Health and Illness Monograph*, 30 (6), 856–68.

(2008b) What are health identities and how may we study them? *Sociology of Health and Illness*, 30 (7), 1007–21.

(2008c) You are what you eat? Vegetarianism, health and identity. *Social Science and Medicine*, 66 (12), 2585–95.

(2008d) Health, ethics and environment: a qualitative study of vegetarian motivations. *Appetite*, 50 (2–3), 422–9.

Fox, N. J., Ward, K. J. and O'Rourke, A. J. (2005a) The 'expert patient': empowerment or medical dominance? the case of Xenical, weight loss and the internet. *Social Science and Medicine*, 16 (6), 1299–1309.

(2005b) Pro-anorexia, weight-loss drugs and the internet: an 'anti-recovery' explanatory model of anorexia. *Sociology of Health and Illness*, 27 (7), 944–71.

(2005c) The birth of the e-clinic. Continuity or transformation in the UK governance of pharmaceutical consumption? *Social Science and Medicine*, 61 (7), 1474–84.

Freidson, E. (1983) Theory of the professions: the state of the art. In Dingwall, R. and Lewis, P. (eds) *Sociology of the Professions*. London: Macmillan.

Freud, S. (1957) Thoughts for the times on war and death. In Strachey, J. (ed.) *Standard Edition of the Complete Psychological Works of Sigmund Freud, Volume XIV*. London: Hogarth Press, pp. 273–300.

(1973) *New Introductory Lectures on Psychoanalysis*. Harmondsworth: Penguin.

Freund, P. E. S., McGuire, M. B. and Podhurst, L. S. (2003) *Health, Illness and the Social Body*. Upper Saddle River, NJ: Prentice Hall.

Fuller, S. (2011) *Humanity 2.0: The Past, Present and Future of What It Means to Be Human*. London: Palgrave Macmillan.

Gagnon, J. H. and Simon, W. (2005) *Sexual Conduct: the Social Sources of Human Sexuality*. Piscataway, NJ: Transaction Publishers.

Gard, M. and Wright, J. (2005) *The Obesity Epidemic: Science, Morality and Ideology*. London: Routledge.

Gardner, K. (1992) The historical conflict between caring and professionalisation: a dilemma for nursing. In Gaut, D. A. (ed.) *The Presence of Caring*. New York: National League for Nursing Press.

Garfinkel, H. (1967) *Studies in Ethnomethodology*. Englewood Cliffs, NJ: Prentice Hall.

Gastaldo, D. (1997) Is health education good for you? Re-thinking health education through the concept of 'biopower'. In Petersen, A. and Bunton, R. (eds) *Foucault, Health and Medicine*. London: Routledge, pp. 113–33.

Gibson, H. B. (2000) It keeps me going. *Ageing and Society*, 20, 773–9.

Glassner, B. (1989) Fitness and the postmodern self. *Journal of Health and Social Behaviour*, 30, 180–91.

Goffman, E. (1968) *Asylums*. Harmondsworth: Penguin.

(1970) *Stigma*. Harmondsworth: Penguin.

(1990) *The Presentation of Self in Everyday Life*. London: Penguin.

Gordo Lopez, A. J. and Cleminson, R. M. (2004) *Techno-sexual Landscapes. Changing Relations between Technology and Sexuality*. London: Free Association Books.

Gordon, T., Holland, J. and Lahelma, E. (2000) Moving bodies/still bodies: embodiment and agency in schools. In McKie, L. and Watson, N. (eds) *Organizing Bodies. Policy, Institutions and Work*. Basingstoke: Macmillan, pp. 81–101.

Gott, M. (2006) Sexual health and the new ageing. *Age and Ageing*, 35 (2), 106–7.

Gott, M. and Hinchliff, S. (2003) How important is sex in later life? The views of older people. *Social Science and Medicine*, 56 (8), 1617–28.

Graham, H. (1979) Prevention and health: every mother's business: a comment on child health policies in the '70s. In Harris, C. C. (ed.) *The Sociology of the Family*. (Sociological Review Monograph 28. Keele: University of Keele.

Graham, H. and Oakley, A. (1986) Ideologies of reproduction. In Currer, C. and Stacey, M. (eds) *Concepts of Health and Illness and Disease: a Comparative Perspective*. Leamington Spa: Berg.

Gray, G. and Pratt, R. (1991) (eds) *Towards a Discipline of Nursing*. Melbourne: Churchill Livingstone.

Greer, G. (1971) *The Female Eunuch*. London: MacGibbon and Kee.

Haraway, D. (1991) *Cyborgs, Simians and Women*. London: Free Association Books.

Hart, R. J. and McKinnon, A. (2010) Sociological epistemology, Durkheim's paradox and Dorothy E Smith's actuality. *Sociology*, 44 (6), 1038–54.

Helman, C. G. (1978) 'Feed a cold, starve a fever': folk models of infection in an English suburban community, and their relation to medical treatment. *Culture, Medicine and Psychiatry*, 2, 107–37.

(1992) Heart disease and the cultural construction of time. In Frankenberg, R. (ed.) *Time, Health and Medicine*. London: Sage.

Henry, D. and Lexchin, J. (2002) The pharmaceutical industry as a medicines provider. *Lancet*, 360, 1590–5.

Herrlinger R. and Feiner E. (1964) Why did Vesalius not discover the fallopian tubes? *Medical History*, 8, 335–41.

Hines, M. (2006) Prenatal testosterone and gender-related behaviour. *European Journal of Endocrinology*, 155 (Supplement 1), S115–S121.

Hird, M. J. (2000) Gender's nature: intersexuality, transsexualism and the 'sex'/'gender' binary. *Feminist Theory*, 1 (3), 347–64.

Hochschild, A. R. (1979) Emotion work, feeling rules and social structure. *American Journal of Sociology*, 85 (3), 551–75.

House, J. S., Landis, K. R. and Umberson, D. (1988) Social relationships and health. *Science*, 241 (4865), 540–5.

Hugman, R. (1991) *Power in Caring Professions*. Basingstoke: Macmillan.

Huijer, M. (1999) The aesthetics of existence in the work of Michel Foucault. *Philosophy and Social Criticism*, 25 (2), 61–85.

Illich, I. (1976) *Limits to Medicine: Medical Nemesis – The Expropriation of Health*. Harmondsworth: Penguin.

Inglesby, E. (1992) Values and philosophy of nursing. The dynamic of change. In Jolley, M. and Brykczynska, G. (eds) *Nursing Care the Challenge to Change*. London: Edward Arnold.

Jackson, S. and Scott, S. (2010) Rehabilitating interactionism for a feminist sociology of sexuality. *Sociology*, 44 (5), 811–26.

James, N. (1989) Emotional labour: skill and work in the social regulation of feelings. *Sociological Review*, 37, 15–42.

Jenkins, R. (1996) *Social Identity*. London: Routledge.

Kinmonth, A. L., Woodcock, A., Griffin, S. et al. (1998) Randomised controlled trial of patient centred care of diabetes in general practice: Impact on current well-being and future disease risk. *British Medical Journal*, 317, 1202–8.

Kirton, M. J. (1994) *Adaptors and Innovators: Styles of Creativity and Problem-Solving*. London: Routledge.

Kleinman, A. (1978) Concepts and a model for the comparison of medical systems as cultural systems. *Social Science and Medicine*, 12, 85–93.

(1980) *Patients and Healers in the Context of Culture*. Berkeley, CA: University of California Press.

(1988) *The Illness Narratives*. New York: Basic Books.

Kleinman, A., Eisenberg, L. and Good, B. (2006) Culture, illness, and care: clinical lessons from anthropologic and cross-cultural research. *Focus: the Journal of Lifelong Learning in Psychiatry*, 4 (1), 140–9.

Kristeva, J. (1986) *The Kristeva Reader*. New York: Columbia University Press.

Latimer, J. (2000) *The Conduct of Care*. Oxford: Blackwell Science.

Le Breton, D. (2004) Genetic fundamentalism or the cult of the gene. *Body and Society*, 10 (4), 1–20.

Lehoux, P., Saint-Arnaud, J. and Richard, L. (2004) The use of technology at home: what patient manuals say and sell vs. what patients face and fear. *Sociology of Health and Illness*, 26 (5), 617–44.

Levin, D. M. and Solomon, G. F. (1990) The discursive formation of the body in the history of medicine. *Journal of Medicine and Philosophy*, 15 (5), 515–37.

Lexchin, J. (2001) Lifestyle drugs: issues for debate. *Canadian Medical Association Journal*, 164 (10), 1449–51.

Lloyd, L. (1999) The wellbeing of carers. In Daykin, N. and Doyal, L. (eds) *Health and Work*. Basingstoke: Macmillan.

Macedo, A., Farré, M. and Baños, J. E. (2003) Placebo effect and placebos: what are we talking about? Some conceptual and historical considerations. *European Journal of Clinical Pharmacology*, 59 (4), 337–42.

Machin, S. and Vignoles, A. (2005) *Education Policy in the UK*. London: Centre for the Economics of Education.

Mackintosh, M. (1979) Domestic labour and the household. In Burman, S. (ed.) *Fit Work for Women*. London: Croom Helm.

McCormack, M. and Anderson, E. (2010) 'It's just not acceptable any more': the erosion of homophobia and the softening of masculinity at an English sixth form. *Sociology*, 44 (5), 843–59.

Manske, P. R. (2007) Medical journal writing. *Journal of Hand Therapy*, 20 (1), 108–12.

Marshall, B. L. (2002) 'Hard science': gendered constructions of sexual dysfunction in the 'Viagra age'. *Sexualities*, 5 (2), 131–58.

Marx, K. (1951) *Value, Price and Profit: Addressed to Working Men*. London: Allen and Unwin.

Marx, K. and Engels, F. (2009) *The Communist Manifesto*. Washington, DC: Regnery Publications.

Massumi, B. (1992) *A User's Guide to Capitalism and Schizophrenia*. Cambridge, Mass: MIT Press.

Mendelson, C. (2003) Gentle hugs: Internet listservs as sources of support for women with lupus. *Advances in Nursing Science*, 26 (4), 299–306.

Mennell, S. (1991) On the civilizing of appetite. In Featherstone, M., Hepworth, M. and Turner, B. S. (eds) *The Body*. London: Sage, pp. 126–56.

Merleau-Ponty, M. (2002) *Phenomenology of Perception*. London: Routledge.

Mitchell, C. (2003) Autism e-mailing lists. *Health Information on the Internet*, 33, 3–4.

Monaghan, L. (2000) Drug-taking, 'risk boundaries' and social identity: bodybuilders talk about Ephedrine and Nubain. *Sociological Research Online*, 5 (2). Accessed at: http://www/socresonline.org.uk/5/2/monaghan.html

Morgan, G. (1997) *Images of Organization*. Thousand Oaks, CA: Sage.

Morris, D. B. (2000) *Illness and Culture in the Postmodern Age*. Berkeley: University of California Press.

Muir Gray, J. A. and Rutter, H. (2002) *The Resourceful Patient*. Oxford: eRosetta Press.

Neal, S. (2000) Feared and revered: media representations of racialized and gendered bodies – a case study. In McKie, L. and Watson, N. (eds) *Organizing Bodies. Policy, Institutions and Work*. Basingstoke: Macmillan, pp. 102–16.

Negrin, L. (2002) Cosmetic surgery and the eclipse of identity. *Body and Society*, 8 (4), 21–42.

Nettleton, S. (1992) *Power, Pain and Dentistry*. Buckingham: Open University Press.

(1997) Governing the risky self; how to be healthy, wealthy, and wise. In Petersen, A. and Bunton, R. (eds) *Foucault, Health and Medicine*. London: Routledge, pp. 207–22.

Nettleton, S. and Watson, J. (1998) *The Body in Everyday Life*. London: Routledge.

Newman, R. (2006) 'Let's just say it works for me'. Rafael Palmeiro, major league baseball, and the marketing of Viagra. *NINE: A Journal of Baseball History and Culture*, 14 (2), 1–14.

NICE (2006) *Clinical Guideline 43: Obesity*. London: National Institute for Health and Clinical Excellence.

Nuland, S. B. (1994) *How we Die*. London: Chatto and Windus.

Oakley, A. (1980) *Women Confined*. Oxford: Martin Robertson.

Ogden, J. (1995) Psychosocial theory and the creation of the risky self. *Social Science and Medicine*, 40 (3), 409–15.

Parker, J. (1999) Nursing as art and science. In Daly, J., Speedy, S. and Jackson, D. (eds) *Contexts of Nursing*. Chatswood, NSW: Churchill Livingstone.

Parsons, T. and Bales, R. (1956) *Family, Socialization and the Interaction Process*. London: Routledge and Kegan Paul.

Parsons, T. and Fox, R. (1952) Illness, therapy, and the modern urban American family. *Journal of Social Issues*, 8 (4), 31–44.

Petersen, A. (1997) Risk, governance and the new public health. In Petersen, A. and Bunton, R. (eds) *Foucault, Health and Medicine*. London: Routledge, pp. 189–206.

(2002) Replicating our bodies, losing our selves: new media portrayals of human cloning in the wake of Dolly. *Body and Society*, 8 (4), 71–90.

Pinder, R. (1992) Coherence and incoherence: doctors' and patients' perspectives on the diagnosis of Parkinson's Disease. *Sociology of Health and Illness*, 14 (1), 1–14.

Popper, K. (1959) Science: conjectures and refutations. In Popper, K. *Conjectures and Refutations*. New York: Basic Books.

Porter, R. (1997) *The Greatest Benefit to Mankind. A Medical History of Humanity from Antiquity to the Present*. London: HarperCollins.

Potts, A. (2004) Deleuze on Viagra (Or, what can a Viagra-body do?). *Body and Society*, 10 (1), 17–36.

Prior, L. (1987) Policing the dead: a sociology of the mortuary. *Sociology*, 21, 355–76.

Prout, A. (1996) Actor-network theory, technology and medical sociology: an illustrative analysis of the metered dose inhaler. *Sociology of Health and Illness*, 18 (2), 198–219.

Rose, N. (1989) *Governing the Soul*. London: Routledge.

(1999) *Powers of Freedom: Reframing Political Thought*. Cambridge: Cambridge University Press.

Rushton, C. H., Sellers, D. E., Heller, K. S. et al. (2009) Impact of a contemplative end-of-life training program: being with dying. *Palliative and Supportive Care*, 7 (4), 405–14.

Rutter, M. (1985) Family and school influences on behavioural development. *Journal of Child Psychology and Psychiatry*, 26, 349–68.

Sackett, D. L., Rosenberg, W. M., Gray, J. A., Haynes, R. B. and Richardson, W. S. (1996) Evidence based medicine: what it is and what it isn't. *British Medical Journal*, 312 (7023), 71–2.

Sairam, K., Kulinskaya, E., Hanbury, D. et al. (2002) Oral sildenafil (Viagra) in male erectile dysfunction: use, efficacy and safety profile in an unselected cohort presenting to a British district general hospital. *BMC Urology*, 2, 4.

Sandelowski, M. (1997) (Ir)reconcilable differences? The debate concerning nursing and technology. *Journal of Nursing Scholarship*, 29 (2), 169–74.

Sapolsky, R. M. (1998) *The Trouble with Testosterone, and Other Essays on the Biology of the Human Predicament*. New York: Touchstone.

Savage, M. (2000) *Class Analysis and Social Transformation*. London: Open University Press.

Scharff, C. (2010) Young women's negotiations of heterosexual conventions: theorizing sexuality in constructions of 'the feminist.' *Sociology*, 44 (5), 827–42.

Scheper-Hughes, N. and Lock, M. (1987) The mindful body: a prolegomenon to future work in medical anthropology. *Medical Anthropology Quarterly*, 1 (1), 6–41.

Schwartz, M. B., O'Neal, H., Brownell, K. D., Blair, S. and Billington, C. (2003) Weight bias among health professionals specializing in obesity. *Obesity Research*, 11, 1033–9.

Seale, C. F. (1998) *Constructing Death: the Sociology of Dying and Bereavement*. Cambridge: Cambridge University Press.

Shakespeare, J., Neve, E. and Hodder, K. (2000) Is norethisterone a lifestyle drug? Results of database analysis. *British Medical Journal*, 320, 291.

Shaw, J. and Baker, M. (2004) Expert patient: dream or nightmare? *British Medical Journal*, 328, 723–4.

Shildrick, M. (1996) Posthumanism and the monstrous body. *Body and Society*, 2 (1), 1–15.

Shilling, C. (1991) Educating the body: physical capital and the production of social inequalities. *Sociology*, 25, 653–72.

Shrock, R. A. (1982) Is health visiting a profession? *Health Visitor*, 55 (3), 104–6.

Sims, S. E. R. (1991) The nature and relevance of theory for practice. In Gray, G. and Pratt, R. (eds) *Towards a Discipline of Nursing*. Melbourne: Churchill Livingstone.

Steinke, E. A. (1994) Knowledge and attitudes of older adults about sexuality in ageing: a comparison of two studies. *Journal of Advanced Nursing*, 19, 477–85.

Strickland, L. A. and DeSpelder, L. A. (2003) Communicating about death and dying. In Corless, I., Germino, B. B. and Pittman, M. A. (eds) *Dying, Death and Bereavement. A Challenge for Living*. New York: Springer.

Strumpf, N. E. and Stevenson, C. M. (1992) Breaking new ground in elder care practice, research and education. In Aiken, L. and Fagin, C. (eds) *Charting Nursing's Future*. Philadelphia: JB Lippincott.

Sudnow, D. (1967) *Passing On: The Social Organization of Dying*. Englewood Cliffs, NJ: Prentice Hall.

Synnott, A. (1993) *The Body Social*. London: Routledge.

Szasz, T. S. and Hollender, M. H. (1956) A contribution to the philosophy of medicine: the basic models of the doctor–patient relationship. *Archives of Internal Medicine*, 97 (585), 592.

Thomas, C. (1993) Deconstructing concepts of care. *Sociology*, 27, 649–70.

Thomas, J. and Dolan, B. (1993) The changing face of nursing 2000 and beyond. In Dolan, B. (ed.) *Project 2000: Reflection and Celebration*. London: Scutari.

Tomasini, F. (2009) Embodying loss and the puzzle of existence. In Latimer, J. and Schillmeier, M. (eds) *Un/knowing Bodies*. Oxford: Blackwell.

Tooby, J. and Cosmides, L. (2005) Conceptual foundations of evolutionary psychology. In Buss, D. (ed.) *The Handbook of Evolutionary Psychology*. Hoboken, NJ: Wiley, pp. 5–67.

Townsend, P. and Davidson, N. (1990) *Inequalities in Health. The Black Report*. Harmondsworth: Penguin.

Tuckett, D., Boulton, M., Olson, C. and Williams, A. (1985) *Meetings Between Experts*. London: Tavistock.

Turner, A. J. and Coyle, A. (2000) What does it mean to be a donor offspring? The identity experiences of adults conceived by donor insemination and the implications for counselling and therapy. *Human Reproduction*, 15 (9), 2041–51.

Turner, B. (1992) *Regulating Bodies*. London: Routledge.

Twigg, J. (2000) Carework as a form of bodywork. *Ageing and Society*, 20 (4), 389–411.

van Gennep, A. (2004) *The Rites of Passage* (translated by Vizedom, M. B. and Caffee, G. I. London: Routledge.

Villaran, C., O'Neill, S. J., Helbling, A. et al. (1999) Montelukast versus salmeterol in patients with asthma and exercise induced bronchoconstriction. *Journal of Allergy and Clinical Immunology*, 104, 547–53.

Walters, A. J. (1995) Technology and the lifeworld of critical care nursing. *Journal of Advanced Nursing*, 22 (2), 338–46.

Watson, J. D. (1968) *The Double Helix*. New York: Mentor (New American Library).

Watson, J. D. and Crick, F. H. C. (1953) A structure for deoxyribose nucleic acid. *Nature*, 171, 737–8.

Watts, M. S. (1975) Editorial: The changing role of the patient. *The Western Journal of Medicine*, 122 (6), 496–7.

Weber, M. (1971) *The Protestant Ethic and the Spirit of Capitalism*. London: Unwin University Books.

WHO (1985) *Targets for Health for All*. Geneva: World Health Organization.

Williams, S. and Bendelow, G. (1998a) *The Lived Body: Sociological Themes, Embodied Issues*. London: Routledge.

(1998b) In search of the missing body: pain, suffering and the post-modern condition. In Scambler, G. and Higgs, P. (eds) *Modernity, Medicine and Health*. London: Routledge, pp. 125–46.

Williams, S. J., Seale, C., Boden, S. et al. (2008) Waking up to sleepiness: Modafinil, the media and the pharmaceuticalisation of everyday/night life. *Sociology of Health and Illness*, 30 (6), 839–55.

Wilson, P. M. (2001) A policy analysis of the expert patient in the United Kingdom: self-care as an expression of pastoral power? *Health and Social Care in the Community*, 9 (3), 134–42.

Witz, A. (2000) Whose body matters? Feminist sociology and the corporeal turn in sociology and feminism. *Body and Society*, 6 (2), 1–24.

Wright, W. (1982) *The Social Logic of Health*. New Brunswick: Rutgers University Press.

Zerubavel, I. (1979) *Patterns of Time in Hospital Life*. Chicago: Chicago University Press.

Zola, I. K. (1966) Culture and symptoms: an analysis of patients presenting complaints. *American Sociological Review*, 31, 615–30.

# Index